WHY DISTANCE LEARNING?
Higher Education Administrative Practices

Gary A. Berg

Foreword by Jack H. Schuster

AMERICAN COUNCIL ON EDUCATION
PRAEGER
Series on Higher Education

Library of Congress Cataloging-in-Publication Data

Berg, Gary A.
   Why distance learning? : higher education administrative practices / Gary A.
Berg ; foreword by Jack H. Schuster.
      p.   cm.—(American Council on Education/Oryx Press series on higher
   education)
   Includes bibliographical references and index.
   ISBN 1–57356–530–X (alk. paper)
   1. Distance education—United States—Administration.   2. Education,
Higher—United States—Administration.   I. Title.   II. Series.
LC5805.B47   2002
378.1′ 75—dc21   2002022445

Formerly ACE/Oryx Press Series on Higher Education

British Library Cataloguing in Publication Data is available.

Copyright © 2002 by American Council on Education and Praeger Publishers

Library of Congress Catalog Card Number: 2002022445
ISBN: 1–57356–530–X

First published in 2002

Praeger Publishers, 88 Post Road West, Westport, CT 06881
An imprint of Greenwood Publishing Group, Inc.
www.praeger.com

Printed in the United States of America

The paper used in this book complies with the
Permanent Paper Standard issued by the National
Information Standards Organization (Z39.48–1984).

10 9 8 7 6 5 4 3 2 1

For my family: Linda, Alec, and Laura

CONTENTS

FOREWORD

G ary Berg's probing examination of the reasons colleges and universities take the plunge into distance learning could hardly be more timely, especially in view of higher education's turbulence—and the crucial role that instructional technology plays in fueling rapid change.

This context—higher education's uncertainty-laced environment—is important. Indeed, American higher education is currently being buffeted by the most rapid sweeping changes in its nearly four-century span. Among the developments driving those changes, none is more powerful than the IT revolution. It is perhaps not the most *abrupt* change, however. Having long taught a seminar on the history of higher education, I believe that the impact of the Serviceman's Readjustment Act of 1944—the GI Bill—caused more convulsions more rapidly as American colleges and universities struggled to absorb a flood of returning veterans. This task was made yet more challenging because these "freshmen" were so strikingly different from prewar collegians. Even so, the system stabilized rather quickly as the tidal wave of veterans receded. Although the long-term influences of the GI "invasion" were to be far reaching (and very positive), it took years before the higher education system embraced the new values associated with teaching a more diverse, more mature clientele. I can think of no other landmark event of comparable immediate effect—not the first Morrill Act of 1862, not the Higher Education Act of 1965, nor even the

Civil Rights Movement or the Women's Movement. All have served to re-shape higher education, but the effects of each developed gradually.

The context now is different, however. It is hard to quarrel with Heraclitus's dictum that the only constant is change; indeed, higher educa-tion, like all else, is always in flux. But never have so many major variables been in motion at the same time. The litany of challenges is familiar: con-strained resources (albeit hardly unusual); intensifying pressures on institu-tions of higher learning to demonstrate their effectiveness; corresponding major shifts in how quality assurance/accreditation is conducted; escalat-ing internationalization of higher education; a stunning transformation in the types of academic appointments being made (away from traditional tenure-track positions toward off-track term appointments); the adminis-tration of universities tilting heavily toward a "management model"; a re-examination, in some venues, of the appropriateness—indeed, the legality—of "affirmative action" and the consequent recalibration of ad-missions and employment policies. And pervading the higher education enterprise is the challenge of how to absorb hundreds of thousands of addi-tional students, both traditional and nontraditional, in the proximate fu-ture—albeit a challenge unevenly distributed geographically. In sum, perhaps never so much has been "in play."

All of the above would constitute a sufficiently daunting higher educa-tion agenda, sweeping higher education downstream in a torrent of white-water, even in the absence of the ongoing technological revolution. But the revolution proceeds apace, permeating and accelerating all the other dimensions of change.

Many—maybe most—colleges and universities have made strategic de-cisions in recent years to bet on distance learning to further their institu-tional aims. But why have they done so? How much can an institution's explanation—that is, its own rhetoric—be trusted as to whether changes in modes of delivering its courses are fundamentally for educational—or other—purposes?

Gary Berg's contribution is significant, for he penetrates the façade and thereby provides more realistic insights into the complex reasons colleges and universities of all types are making major commitments to distance learning. His access to instructional technology's institutional leaders has yielded many candid comments about the mix of reasons—reasons that span visions of financial sugar plums to basic philosophical commitments to the importance of expanding access. In the process of exploring those reasons, the reader will acquire insights into the exciting educational di-mensions of IT, as well as be exposed to some sobering realities. In all, no one as yet has succeeded as well as Dr. Berg in dissecting the motivations that continue to propel the IT revolution. His careful documentation and analysis enable the reader—both the IT specialist and the higher education generalist—to reach a better understanding of this remarkable phenomenon that is so profoundly reshaping higher education and to speculate more intelligently about what the future of IT may hold.

Jack H. Schuster

ACKNOWLEDGMENTS

This book could not have been written without the contribution of many people who influenced the direction of my research. I'd like to thank Jack Schuster, Daryl Smith and Phil Dreyer at Claremont Graduate University for their guidance throughout the process of writing. I need especially to thank Jack Schuster for his advice, encouragement and support in finding a publisher. He continually pushed me to do more than simply present the data, to express my opinions and make suggestions that might be helpful to practitioners in the field. With some reluctance, because of the newness and the controversial nature of the field, I have done so.

In addition, I want to thank Jeanne Nakamura for her early comments on my proposal, especially to broaden the inquiry so that I could use the data for multiple research purposes. This has resulted in another book, *The Knowledge Medium: Designing Effective Computer Learning Environments*, centering on pedagogical issues. Some of the ideas presented in this book have appeared in early form in various publications. I'd like to acknowledge the following publications for their initial support of my scholarship in this field: *WebNet Journal: Internet Technologies, Applications & Issues, Journal of Educational Multimedia and Hypermedia, Education at a Distance Journal, Journal of Asynchronous Learning Networks*, and *Education Policy Analysis Archives*. In the latter stages of completing this book, Betty C. Pessagno, senior production editor, and copyeditor Barbara Goodhouse offered many useful suggestions for improving the overall readability of the manuscript. Finally, I want to thank my wife, Linda Venis, for her expert editing and useful reflections on the book as a higher education administrator.

INTRODUCTION

... educational innovations are almost never installed on their merits. Characteristics of the local system, of the innovating person or group, and of other relevant groups often outweigh the impact of what the innovative action is.

(Miles, 1964, p. 635)

Does distance learning in higher education represent an innovation? How do universities regard it? Are there aspects of distance learning that explain the reasons for the implementation in American higher education that have little or nothing to do with merit? As the quotation above suggests, it may not necessarily matter whether or not distance learning is actually an innovation in higher education in terms of why it is being implemented. What may be more crucial in implementation decisions are the connotations and meaning attached to distance learning in given academic cultures.

Why are higher education institutions venturing into the use of alternative delivery formats of learning? A. W. (Tony) Bates (2000b) sees higher education institutions as being motivated by various factors, including the desire to improve the quality of learning, provide students with information technology (IT) skills needed for the future, widen access, respond to a perceived technological imperative, and reduce the cost of education. How do these differing motivations affect the administration, management, and course development process? To what degree is the influence of corporate approaches on administration shaping the way distance learning in higher education is implemented and managed? Furthermore, how is the presence of such influences affecting the development of new pedagogical approaches to the use of educational technology?

Ehrmann (1998) identifies common institutional motives for the use of distance learning as widening access, sharing a wider range of intellectual resources, and implementing new teaching techniques. Given these motives, he sees the challenge as extending access and updating and enriching resources, while at the same time controlling costs. Whether the motive is to widen access, share intellectual resources, or implement new teaching techniques, the reasons for universities to use technology need to be clarified and the subsequent ramifications on practices understood. In the 1999 *Distance Education Handbook* of the Accrediting Commission for Community and Junior Colleges of the Western Association of Schools and Colleges, motivation is listed as the first element to consider for institutions using and developing distance learning programs:

> The institution should examine closely its motivation for doing distance education, since the driving forces behind this effort are many—the potential for increasing enrollment, public pressure, reducing cost, grant monies, opportunities for faculty to be creative, notions that everybody-is-doing-it, and many more. Lack of an identified need for distance learning, whether real or perceived, can influence achievement of institutional understanding of the motives for doing distance education. Understanding institutional motives can drive institutional commitment to the program, an essential matter if students are to be ensured the opportunity to complete educational goals in such a program. (Accrediting Commission for Community and Junior Colleges, Western Association of Schools and Colleges, 1999, p. 1)

According to Bates (2000b), the effective use of technology requires a revolution in thinking about teaching and learning, and necessitates restructuring the way universities are planned, managed, and organized. The challenge universities face is in clarifying their goals in the use of technology, and then understanding the long-term implications. This study is an attempt to see how universities are meeting this challenge.

This book attempts to address the following research questions: Why are higher education institutions venturing into the use of distance learning? How do these differing motivations affect administration and management practices? How are motivations affecting the manner in which pedagogical issues are addressed? To what degree is the influence of corporate approaches to administration shaping the way distance learning in higher education is implemented and managed?

In addition to the research questions, I put forward the following tentative propositions to test: Distance learning format courses are implemented in higher education primarily in order to increase revenue. There is a relationship between institutional motives to increase revenue and a lack of pedagogical sophistication in distance learning format courses. Institutions implementing distance learning primarily in order to increase revenue are less likely to have high academic standards.

Before going further, it is important to clarify definitions of the field. On an international scale there are probably as many different terms and phrases used for distance learning as there are different combinations of delivery systems. "Distance learning" is a generic term that includes the range of teaching/learning strategies variously referred to as correspondence education, correspondence study, home study, independent study, distance learning, computer-assisted learning, online learning, and distance education. Related terms such as open learning, nontraditional studies, outreach, distributed learning, and off-campus programs also appear in the literature. The term "open and distant learning" (ODL) is used in the United Kingdom in connection with the various British Open University approaches (Tait, 1999). "Distance education" has been used as the general term for this whole area of education. In 1994 the National Home Study Council (NHSC), established in 1926, changed its name to the Distance Education and Training Council (DETC) because of the manner in which members were delivering education. According to DETC, distance education provides lesson materials prepared for study by learners on their own (Spille, Stewart & Sullivan, 1997). "Distance teaching" refers generally to the institutional role of providing education at a distance.

It is a common experience for those studying the field to get bogged down in definitions connected to specific technologies. I want to avoid this approach. As Kidwell, Mattie, and Sousa (2000) argue, it is a problem to define distance learning by specific technologies because the technologies, and consequently the definition, become obsolete very quickly. Additionally, it is an assumption of this study that the technology is less important than the attitudes, approaches, and management patterns of distance learning in higher education.

"Distance learning" is used in this study because it emphasizes the recentering on the nontraditional learner and is more commonly used than "distance education." As this study focuses on administrative issues in connection with the use of distance learning in higher education, the primary aspects of my definition for the study have this focus. For the purposes of this study, I suggest that the main elements of distance learning are:

- physical separation (complete or more than 50% reduced contact time) between teacher and learner;
- administration by an educational organization;
- frequent use of various media, including print, video, film, computer, and audio;
- communication between student and teacher, synchronous or asynchronous;
- often an administrative focus on the nontraditional learner.

The overall plan for this book is to first review relevant research literatures, describe the research methods, and then present and analyze the results. Reviews of the research literature serve to identify gaps in previous research and help to refine the research questions (Marshall & Rossman, 1989). In Chapter 1, related surveys of universities regarding distance learning practices are examined to understand methods previously applied and gaps in knowledge. In Chapter 2, research literature on historical and current approaches to the management of distance learning programs in higher education is reviewed in order to better interpret the data collected. In Chapter 3, the emerging research and theory of the pedagogy of distance learning are summarized to analyze the level of sophistication individual institutions are using in their own approach. In Chapter 4, literature on the use of market models in the university, or what is sometimes called "academic capitalism," is reviewed to help identify the ways in which distance learning relates to this trend. Chapter 5 details the research methods used for this study. Chapters 6, 7, 8, and 9 present the results in relationship to institutional motive, evidence of commercialization, and effect on levels of pedagogical sophistication. In Chapter 10 conclusions are drawn from the results of the research.

I want to summarize my research findings and preview some of the themes in what is to come. The study found that explicit reasons for using distance learning focused primarily on access, while the second most common response was a belief in the pedagogical advantages of distance learning. Nevertheless, indications of a connection between distance learning and the commercialization of higher education were found in the following data: top university and continuing education administrators led the implementation push for distance learning more than twice as often as individual faculty; distance learning is primarily administratively housed in self-supporting continuing education units; the majority of respondents pay full-time faculty under a regular load arrangement for distance learning courses, with no additional stipend for course development; and most respondents say institutions own distance learning intellectual property. Additionally, it was found that community colleges have different attitudes toward distance learning than doctoral degree–granting institutions, the former focusing more on access and providing information technology skills, while research institutions responded more often that they develop distance learning programs with explicit revenue motivations. In terms of pedagogy, only slight indications were found that the pursuit of revenue affects both teaching/learning and academic quality. Those showing a concern for access rather than the pursuit of new sources of revenue indicate slightly higher (but statistically not significant) sophistication in pedagogical approach. Additionally, those institutions with a revenue motive in comparison to those motivated by access issues more often responded that they take less than six months to develop a course and less often look at developing course materials specifically suited to distance learning formats.

The first theme is that I have found, not surprisingly, that faculty members are a key in what I would describe as an evolutionary process of distance learning in America. Probably the single most startling discovery I have made is that such a high percentage of regular faculty teach distance learning courses. There are two main issues here: first, if regular faculty simply convert their courses to computer-based platforms, we are only automating, not innovating. Second, if we rely on full-time faculty for academic quality in distance learning courses, what happens in the likely scenario when part-time faculty are brought in to teach these courses?

The second theme I want to suggest up front is that there are indications that distance learning is pursued by some institutions (particularly doctoral degree–granting institutions) as a way of generating new revenue. While this pushes us into a larger debate about the commercialization of higher education usually concentrating on corporate-funded research, the distance learning portion is crucial because it impacts the central function of education: teaching/learning. For this reason I think it is time for a collective ethical gut check in higher education. Do we pursue distance learning because it offers the opportunity for greater financial reward, or because it really provides meaningful access? If it does both, how do we assure quality when traditional standards no longer apply?

Finally, I want to reveal early on that what I have uncovered in the writing of this book is a paradox. Distance learning in American higher education is not an isolated phenomenon, but is really at the heart of major changes occurring in the academy. I have found that distance learning, rather than using radically different administrative methods to provide new educational services, is thus far quite traditional in many ways. The paradox is that in my mind this sticking to traditional academic methods is primarily responsible for the baseline level of quality that exists in these programs today. On the other hand, the revolutionary changes in both administrative structure and pedagogy cannot occur when we simply automate the traditional classroom. The main point here is that distance learning will always be a pale imitation of face-to-face learning as long as it attempts little more than to duplicate the classroom. Perhaps this is simply evolution—if so, we have yet to crawl out of the mud at the shoreline.

CHAPTER 1

Review of Surveys on Technology and Distance Learning in Higher Education

This chapter analyzes the limited data currently available on distance learning practices in higher education. Distance learning is defined differently (or not at all) in the various data sources. General surveys include "Campus Computing 1999" (Green, 2000), Dun & Bradstreet Market Data Retrieval Division's "College Technology Review" (2000), "Distance Education: A Planner's Casebook" (Witherspoon, 1997), "Distance Education Profiles: Fifteen Examples of Distance Education Practice" (Witherspoon, 1998), the U.S. Department of Education, National Center for Education Statistics, "Distance Education in Higher Education Institutions" (Lewis, Alexander & Farris, 1997), and "The Survey of Distance Learning Programs in Higher Education" (Primary Research Group, 1999).

"Campus Computing 1999: The Tenth National Survey of Desktop Computing and Information Technology in Higher Education" (Green, 2000) focuses more broadly on the use of technology in higher education, but does include some data relevant to issues of compensation for faculty that give an overview of the institutional trends. The survey was designed to collect information about campus planning, policies, and procedures affecting the use of computers in higher education. A random sample of public and private two- and four-year colleges and universities was conducted. While most of the findings from this survey focus on the broader uses of computer technology in higher education, the study did find low levels of budgetary incentives (approximately 5%) for faculty to use technology in teaching.

Similar in its broad approach to the "Campus Computing" survey, Dun & Bradstreet Market Data Retrieval Division's "College Technology Review" (2000) surveyed the key administrative contacts at accredited two- and four-year colleges across the country to learn the answers to questions such as, How much is being spent on academic and administrative hardware and software? Which schools offer distance learning programs? How many students have Internet access? The study shows that the number of colleges and universities offering distance degree programs more than doubled from the previous year. Seventy-two percent of the 1,028 colleges that answered a question on distance education said they were offering distance-learning programs this year; 34% reported offering a degree. This study does not focus specifically on distance learning, but rather on technology more generally. Primary areas of interest for the study are technology spending and access for students and faculty.

"Distance Education: A Planner's Casebook" (Witherspoon, 1997) provides case information on distance learning programs in specific topical areas such as rural students, cooperative degree programs, and workplace applications. Twenty-three institutions are profiled in connection with these specific issues as case examples of distance learning practice. Case study methods are not published in this report. The findings of this study include principles of good practice.

"Distance Education Profiles" is a 1998 survey conducted by the Western Cooperative for Educational Telecommunications which queries 15 colleges in depth regarding technologies employed, student services, faculty issues, and management. The 15 institutions are meant to represent a mix of institutional types exemplary for their commitment to providing high quality learning experiences. The report ends with a summary analysis revealing consensus points on practices common to many of the respondents, as well as areas where they diverge.

The Primary Research Group survey data are based on a random sample of 61 college and university distance learning programs throughout the United States and Canada. The survey sample included 44 programs in public universities and 17 in independents; 32 programs were at two-year institutions, and 29 at four-year institutions. The data are presented in the aggregate and by type (public/private), level of the college (two-year/four-year), and number of students enrolled in the program. The study found that 86.96% of the programs operate at a profit. Furthermore, 36.68% of the instructors are classified as adjunct, a significant increase over the previous survey in 1998, in which 27.34% had such a classification.

Books cataloguing distance learning programs include *Peterson's Guide to Distance Learning Courses* (University Continuing Education Association [UCEA, 2000]), *Peterson's Independent Study Catalog* (UCEA, 1999), and *Campus-Free College Degrees: Thorson's Guide to Accredited Distance Learning Degree Programs* (Thorson, 1999). Thorson lists 145 accredited institutions offering "campus-free" degree programs through various formats, while UCEA lists 142 accredited institutions offering independent study format courses and over 1,000 institutions practicing distance learning. As these books are catalogues of programs, they offer no research findings.

Surveys relevant to faculty issues include "Faculty Compensation and Support Issues in Distance Education," published by the Instructional Telecommunications Council (ITC) (Edwards & Minich, 1998), and the National Education Association (NEA) survey "Bargaining Technology Issues in Higher Education" (NEA, 1999). The ITC survey is a query of its membership in four main areas: faculty compensation, intellectual property rights, support services, and professional development. As only the membership of ITC was surveyed, this sample is not random. Since the organization focuses on educational telecommunications, there is a clear bias toward video-based courses. Furthermore, 94.7% of the respondents were from community colleges and 97.3% from public institutions. The NEA survey was taken from the 1998–99 release of NEA's Higher Education Contract Analysis System (HECAS), which includes over 500 higher education contracts and has the ability to search on specific words or phrases. Findings from this survey relevant to this book include a pattern of faculty compensated for teaching distance learning format courses through regular load or overload with no additional stipend. Furthermore, 45% of the respondents claim that the institution owns the rights to the distance learning courses.

Another NEA survey, "A Survey of Traditional and Distance Learning Higher Education Members" (NEA, 2000), is based on interviews of 402 distance learning faculty and 130 traditional faculty in early 2000 identifying the strengths and weaknesses of distance teaching and learning. A distance learning course was defined as one in which more than half of the instruction takes place when faculty and students are at different locations and the instruction is delivered through audio, video, or computer technologies. Correspondence courses and traditional courses with a smaller distance learning component were not considered distance learning courses. Three-quarters of the instructors surveyed were positive about distance learning, their views apparently rooted in technology's ability to extend educational opportunities to students who cannot take courses in a traditional setting. This connection of access to distance learning may be heightened by the heavy concentration of community colleges in the NEA membership. Interestingly, it was found that faculty believe they will be hurt financially by distance learning, but the prospect of being able to offer an education to students who could not otherwise enroll in a course outweighs this personal financial concern. In relationship to this book, the NEA survey found that over 50% of the respondents felt that administrators were the most forceful proponent of distance learning. The limitation of this survey is that it focuses completely on NEA members, with a resulting heavy emphasis on community colleges.

"State Policies for Distance Education" (Epper, 1999) is a survey published by State Higher Education Executive Officers (SHEEO), cataloguing state policies on the use of distance education technology. Forty-four states responded to the survey, which identified trends and changes in state policy in light of the increasing number of degree programs offered through distance education technology. Fran Tracy-Mumford, Delaware's director of adult education, conducted a similar survey while she was a National Institute for Literacy Leadership Fellow from 1997 to 1998. A subsequent publication was issued called "How States Are Implementing Distance Education for Adult Learners" (Tracy-Mumford, 2000). Data were updated the following year through a review of state plans and interviews with state directors. The survey looks at state-level use, projected use, and issues. The findings indicate the growing use of distance learning and the still early format of policies for best practices.

"The Teaching, Learning and Computing Survey" (Center for Research on Information Technology and Organizations, 1999) collected data on K–12 teachers from a national sample of 898 public, private, and parochial schools selected from a national database of 109,000 schools and from two targeted samples of schools—high-end technology-using schools and schools that participate in 52 identified national and regional educational reform programs. The Teaching, Learning and Computing study is a research project at the University of California, Irvine, that focuses completely on K–12 pedagogical approaches to the use of technology in the classroom; consequently the findings are not directly relevant to my study.

Although the issue of the relative effectiveness of distance learning and traditional classroom courses is outside the immediate concern of this study, one should note that a number of studies have taken up this issue. A debate on the effectiveness of distance learning has led to numerous studies over the past forty years. *The No Significant Difference Phenomenon* (Russell, 1999) lists over 400 studies that conclude there are no significant differences in learning outcomes when comparing specific distance learning format students to traditional classroom students. In response, the NEA (National Education Association) and AFT (American Federation of Teachers) commissioned the Institute for Higher Education Policy (1999) to examine the quality of the studies listed in Russell's book and to find gaps in the research. Its findings include criticism of the research methods used in many of the studies.

Probably the survey most relevant to this study is the U.S. Department of Education's "Distance Education in Higher Education Institutions" (Lewis, Alexander & Farris, 1997), which found that public policy, legal concerns, lack of support from administration, and lack of fit with institutional mission were seen as "not at all" a deterrent to starting or expanding distance education courses. Furthermore, institutions were asked about the importance of various goals to their distance education program and the extent to which the distance education program is meeting those goals they consider important. Increasing student access was an important goal for most distance education programs. Increasing access by making courses available at convenient locations was rated as very important by 82% of the institutions, and increasing access by reducing time constraints for course taking was rated as very important by 63% of institutions. Making educational opportunities more affordable for students, another aspect of student access, was rated as very important by half of the institutions.

Goals concerning increasing the institution's audiences and enrollments were also perceived as quite important, with increasing access to new audiences and increasing enrollments rated as very important by 64% and 54% of institutions, respectively. Reducing per-student costs, often mentioned in the research literature as an important reason for institutions to offer distance education, was rated as very important by 20% of the institutions. Meeting the needs of local employers was considered a very important goal by 38% of the institutions, and improving the quality of course offerings was considered very important by 46% of the institutions.

The percentage of institutions rating various goals as very important showed some variation by institutional type. Public two-year institutions were more likely than public four-year institutions to perceive the following goals to be very important: reducing per-student costs, making educational opportunities more affordable, increasing institution enrollments, and increasing student access by reducing time constraints. In addition, public two-year institutions were more likely than private four-year institutions to perceive reducing per-student costs and meeting the needs of local employers as very important.

In general in this U.S. Department of Education survey, institutions indicated that most of their goals were met to a minor or moderate extent. Goals particularly likely to be met concerned student access, convenience, and reducing time constraints for course taking. The extent to which institutions believed that they had met various goals varied by how important the particular goal was perceived to be. In general, institutions that perceived a particular goal as very important more frequently indicated that the goal had been met to a moderate or major extent, while institutions that perceived a goal as somewhat important more frequently indicated that the goal had been met to a minor extent. For example, the majority of institutions that perceived making educational opportunities more affordable for students to be a very important goal indicated that the goal had been met to a moderate extent (52%) or major extent (23%). Fifty-nine percent of institutions that perceived this goal to be somewhat important indicated that the goal had been met to a minor extent.

A subsequent 1997–1998 survey was conducted by the National Center for Education Statistics. "Distance Education at Postsecondary Education Institutions: 1997–98" (1997) updated and expanded the information from the original survey. The survey also compared the two surveys and found an increase in distance learning and a stable number of institutions offering distance learning, but a doubling of their offerings. The second survey was slightly altered and dropped the question about institutional reasons for using technology.

In conclusion, one can see from this review that most surveys on distance learning focus on cataloguing programs and measuring growth. Only the U.S. Department of Education survey, "Distance Education in Higher Education Institutions" (Lewis, Alexander & Farris, 1997), specifically looks at the question of institutional motive for using distance learning. Furthermore, none of the studies addresses directly the connection between the commercialization of higher education and distance learning, or the relationship between institutional motive and pedagogical approaches to distance learning. Consequently, the research conducted herein clearly fills a gap in research conducted to date.

CHAPTER

Review of Literature on Administration of Distance Learning in Higher Education

How do differing institutional motivations affect administration and management practices?

This chapter traces the historical development of distance learning in higher education. Additionally, relevant research literature is reviewed on educational change theory in general and as it relates to technology, the role of the faculty, leading models, and the growing best practices literature. The data returned in this study and reported in Chapter 7 indicate how institutional motivation to use distance learning affects specific administrative practices by looking at such issues as course approval process, where courses are administratively housed, faculty compensation practices, partnership agreements, marketing practices, and assessment. Consequently, an understanding of administrative practices in regard to these issues and others is important in evaluating the effect of motivation on them.

CORRESPONDENCE INSTRUCTION

Higher education institutions initially became involved in distance learning (broadly defined) in the United States through correspondence instruction in the late nineteenth century. The first established university to offer correspondence courses was Illinois Wesleyan University, which in 1873 began to offer such courses to supplement the traditional classroom courses that could lead to A.B. or Ph.D. degrees (MacKenzie, Christensen & Rigby, 1968; Rumble & Harry, 1982). In 1883, 32 professors from major universities including Harvard, Johns Hopkins, Cornell, and the University of Wisconsin met to form the Correspondence University with its base of operations in Ithaca, New York. The Correspondence University did not offer separate degrees, and was mostly interested in correspondence courses to supplement the traditional classroom courses (MacKenzie, Christensen & Rigby, 1968; Noffsinger, 1942).

However, the clear leader in correspondence course instruction in higher education was the University of Chicago, led by William Rainey Harper, its first president. Harper's original contact with correspondence instruction was through his role as a language instructor for a summer Chautauqua program. The Chautauqua Movement was a very influential program of adult enrichment that began as a summer Bible study program, but soon blossomed into a larger nontraditional educational program at the end of the nineteenth century in America. The Chautauqua Movement in many ways is at the historical root of many of the innovations in higher education, including university extension, summer sessions, university presses, and distance learning in the form of correspondence courses. Although essentially a noncredit institution conceptually from the beginning, Chautauqua needs to be considered as part of the movement of distance learning because it had such a strong influence on higher education institutions (the University of Chicago in particular), and because it began to offer degree credit in 1883 (Nanson, 1989).

The Chautauqua Movement started in 1874 in a meeting at Lake Chautauqua, New York, organized by Lewis Miller, a manufacturer, and John Heyl Vincent, a Methodist preacher. They were drawn together originally to encourage self-improvement through study of the Bible. Their methods were intensive instruction supplemented with games, lectures, concerts, and even fireworks. The program grew in popularity very quickly. In 1878 Vincent designed a four-year course of guided reading called the Chautauqua Literary and Scientific Circle (CLSC), which could be completed by students on their own throughout the year between in-person summer meetings. Enrollment in the CLSC climbed from 8,400 in the first year to 100,000 in ten years. The support for the Chautauqua program was widespread, cutting across classes, from storekeepers and farmers, to American intellectuals and scientists (interestingly, given his leadership in educational technology, Thomas Edison was a regular participant) (Morrison, 1974; Gould, 1961).

In 1883 a group of Baptists created their own Chautauqua-style retreat directly across the lake, and Vincent responded by luring away one of their most charismatic leaders, William Rainey Harper. Harper began to offer correspondence courses in Hebrew in 1881 to his seminary students because of a lack of adequate facilities to meet student need, and continued this practice at Chautauqua. He was an immediate success as both a teacher and an administrator at Chautauqua, and by 1885 was listed as the principal of the School of Hebrew. Although Anna Ticknor is usually credited with being the first to offer correspondence courses in America, William Rainey Harper was responsible for their widespread acceptance in academia (Morrison, 1974; Gould, 1961).

Vincent visited England in 1886 and was greatly impressed by the University Extension Movement, and this inspired him to enlarge his vision for Chautauqua. He called a meeting and involved Harper that year in his new project to expand. In 1888 a plan for Chautauqua University Extension was created and a pamphlet was distributed that described the new university, which had the following key elements: (1) voluntary association of students; (2) promotion of good citizenship; (3) emphasis on natural science; (4) cooperation with traditional higher education institutions when possible; (5) affiliation with libraries, unions, and guilds; and (6) delivery through lectures, discussions, printed materials, exercises, and examinations offered through locally organized chapters. The university was an immediate success and was only finally supplanted through imitation by traditional higher education institutions, especially the University of Chicago (Gould, 1961; Morrison, 1974).

The New York State legislature recognized Chautauqua courses for degree credit in 1883, but Chautauqua's leaders insisted that their courses were not to replace traditional university education but instead were to lead students into residential education. Indeed, Chautauqua's leaders were quick to admit that their credit was not the same as that of traditional universities. Chautauqua gave up the practice of granting credit in 1898, although the New York State Department of Education still recognized credit from Chautauqua up until 1926 (Gould, 1961; Nanson, 1989).

By 1890 there were 200 independent Chautauquas or imitators of the Chautauqua format all over the country, which taken together created a great shift in America in regard to popular education. One of several waves of mass enthusiasm for self-improvement, social betterment, and reform that have periodically swept over our nation, the Chautauqua Movement left behind changed tastes, changed laws, and changed social habits (Gould, 1961, p. viii). Particularly for Americans in the Midwest and West, the Chautauquas offered a connection to their heritage and the quickly changing modern world identified with the East. The books, lessons, and circles broadened their lives. Chautauqua grew and evolved over the years and survived in various forms up until recent times. Speakers at the annual camp over the years included many American presidents (Gould, 1961).

When Harper went to teach at Yale in 1887, he took the operation of the School of Hebrew with him along with a staff including editors, a business agent, stenographers, correspondence instructors, clerks, a bookkeeper, and part-time student workers (Gould, 1961). Harper spent five years at the Yale Divinity School while still heading the Chautauqua College of Liberal Arts, which became the American Institute of Sacred Literature. In 1892 he became president of the newly formed University of Chicago (MacKenzie, Christensen & Rigby, 1968; Noffsinger, 1942).

Harper's experience through the Chautauqua Movement of seeing thousands of students assembled each summer and continuing through the winter via correspondence impressed upon him America's thirst for knowledge beyond the traditional confines of established contemporary education. Clearly, Harper used many of the innovative ideas from Chautauqua in developing the University of Chicago. When Chicago opened in 1892, it was organized into five divisions based on the Chautauqua model, including the university proper, press, libraries, laboratories and museums, affiliations, and extension, which specifically provided for correspondence instruction.

The development of an extension division was a very innovative notion at the time, one that is difficult to fully appreciate looking back now, when most major universities take continuing education for granted. Harper's experience with correspondence courses through Chautauqua University obviously influenced the creation of the Correspondence Study Department, later renamed the Home-Study Department, at the University of Chicago. In fact, Chautauqua language courses were brought by Harper from Yale and reconstituted by him under the University of Chicago Divinity School banner in 1905 (Reeves, Thompson, Klein & Russell, 1933).

In the first years of operation, the Home-Study Department was very successful. Enrollments in correspondence courses at the University of Chicago increased from 93 in 1892–93 to 1,485 in 1901–2 (Reeves, Thompson, Klein & Russell, 1933). However, as the offering of correspondence courses by other universities became more common, particularly among public institutions, it became difficult for the University of Chicago to compete. In 1925–26 the University of Chicago reached a peak of 10,545 correspondence course enrollments (out of 62,552 nationally), but then began to decline steadily. A fee increase after 1926 is said to have been a factor in the decline in enrollments (Reeves, Thompson, Klein & Russell, 1933). Correspondence courses at the University of Chicago had no internal financial support and therefore had difficulty competing with lower fees from public institutions. The number of universities offering correspondence courses grew from 1 in 1892 to 33 in 1927. At the peak of enrollments in correspondence courses, the University of Chicago was the only large private institution offering credit courses in this format. Its Home-Study Department provided service for 72 years until it closed in 1964 (MacKenzie, Christensen & Rigby, 1968; Noffsinger, 1942). According to Froke (1995), there was mounting antagonism to the correspondence program as the years passed, as regular faculty participation dropped and enrollments declined.

History shows that at the University of Chicago correspondence instruction played an important role in bringing new students to the traditional programs—49% of the students enrolled in correspondence courses went on to receive a degree at the university (Reeves, Thompson, Klein & Russell, 1933). Clearly, correspondence courses brought many benefits to the institution as a whole by recruiting new students to the traditional degree programs and by providing additional income for faculty members.

Although the University of Chicago's home study courses met with some academic criticism for their nontraditional students, other universities imitated the effort. By World War I, more than 12 universities offered a form of correspondence instruction for credit, including Pennsylvania State College, Baylor University, the University of California at Berkeley, the University of Nebraska, and the University of Wisconsin. Lacking a leader with the unique background of Harper, these institutions became involved in correspondence instruction in different ways, and for different reasons. For example, while the University of Wisconsin closely followed the University of Chicago's model, its reason for developing the correspondence course program was reportedly to broaden its curriculum, particularly in relationship to vocational training. Consequently, Wisconsin's correspondence courses were more vocational in nature than the ones at the University of Chicago (MacKenzie, Christensen & Rigby, 1968).

The University of California at Berkeley began its correspondence department in 1913 and by 1964 had the largest university-based program in the country. The University of Nebraska developed a correspondence program similar to Wisconsin's and by 1964 was second to the University of California at Berkeley in annual enrollments (MacKenzie, Christensen &

Rigby, 1968). In 1964, 58 member institutions of the National University Continuing Education Association (NUCEA) offered correspondence instruction (Fleming, 1964). However, none of those universities would allow students to earn a degree completely through correspondence instruction.

EDUCATIONAL FILM/INSTRUCTIONAL FILM

The development of educational technology use in higher education also began at the end of the nineteenth century. Thomas Edison was one of the first to produce films for classroom use. In 1911 he released a series of historical films about the American Revolution, with the first called *The Minute Men*. In 1914 he released a series on natural and physical sciences as well. Many colleges and universities were involved in educational film production as early as the 1910s. Yale University and the University of Minnesota were large players in this early production. The first educational film catalogue in the United States, *Catalogue of Educational Motion Pictures*, was published in 1910 and listed 1,065 titles. Demand for training films during World War I led to an increase in educational film production. However, by the late 1920s and early 1930s, educational film companies had financial troubles (Saettler, 1990).

World War II was a turning point in educational film in terms of both number and technique. The use of educational films was part of the official policy of the War Department, and consequently this led to the production of six times more educational films than had been created up to that point. Film production during the war led to two stylistic or pedagogical improvements mostly brought about by the influx of Hollywood filmmakers into the military: first-person camera angles and camera movement. Further, the military applied dramatic techniques used previously only in entertainment films. After World War II additional universities became involved in educational filmmaking, including the University of Chicago, the University of Southern California, Ohio State University, the University of Wisconsin, New York University, Indiana University, the University of Minnesota, Iowa State University, the University of Michigan, Boston University, and Syracuse University (Saettler, 1990).

The first academic research on instructional films was done in 1912. The first large-scale research was done by Johns Hopkins University in 1919 analyzing the effectiveness of films on venereal disease prevention (Saettler, 1990).

AUDIO RECORDINGS AND RADIO
FOR EDUCATIONAL PURPOSES

Thomas Edison's invention of the tinfoil phonograph in 1877 made the first language laboratories possible. The phonograph was first used in 1891 in a foreign language class offered at the College of Milwaukee. In 1900 a professor at the University of California taught Chinese concurrently at the University of Pennsylvania using a wax cylinder sent across the United States. Thomas J. Foster's International Correspondence Schools used the cylinders for foreign language courses early on as well. The methods and procedures for language correspondence courses were developed in this early period and applied later using more sophisticated technologies, including video and film (Kitao, 1995).

After World War I, university-owned radio stations became a common phenomenon. Educational radio grew greatly from 1925 to 1935, and by 1936 there were 202 such stations across the country. At its height, 36 institutions offered courses combining radio broadcasts and correspondence by mail, 13 for credit (Pittman, 1986). "Schools of the Air" were founded at the University of Wisconsin, Kansas University, the University of Michigan, and the University of Minnesota. At first the courses simply involved professors reading lectures over the radio, but they grew in sophistication and production values (Saettler, 1990). By the end of World War II, all of these efforts were discontinued. Federal regulation, the rise of commercial radio networks, limitations of the broadcast signal, lack of a target population, and minimal faculty involvement were reasons identified for the failure (Saettler, 1990; Pittman, 1986).

EDUCATIONAL AND INSTRUCTIONAL TELEVISION

In the research literature, the term "educational television" usually refers to programs that have a broad cultural purpose, such as *Sesame Street*, while "instructional television" is generally used to describe videotaped whole courses. The first instructional television station began in 1953 at the University of Iowa, and by the 1960s such stations were used widely in the United States. The breakthrough in educational television came with the use of trained staff, faculty used on a rotating basis, improved studio resources, a nationwide network, and commitment by educators to use instructional television. The 1958 National Defense Education Act (NDEA), Title VII, provided for presenting academic subject matter through media and encouraged the development of instructional television (Saettler, 1990). In the 1970s, community colleges developed telecourses to deliver coursework, which have found a steady audience up until the present time. Course developers such as the Public Broadcasting Service (PBS) (funded partly by the Annenberg Foundation), Dallas Telecourses, and Coast Community College District regularly supply course content to other universities through licensing agreements.

In the 1960s researchers began to look for significant differences between instructional television and traditional classroom experiences in terms of learning outcomes. As was noted in the previous chapter, the interpretation of this research is still actively debated today. Saettler (1990) points out that instructional TV was often seen as entertainment and therefore not regarded as part of the regular curriculum. Research on *Sesame Street* showed that educational effectiveness was limited by the absence of support materials and an interested adult to encourage and enrich lessons.

Kent and McNergney (1999) claim that two factors led to the deemphasis of educational and instructional television: lack of quality programming and the teacherless approach to the medium. The teacherless approach does not allow teachers to control or interact with the medium, and students are unable to raise questions or respond to media such as film, radio, and television. Kent and McNergney argue that low technologies such as the chalkboard and textbooks have been more successful because they work in teacher-defined curricula and are more flexible and durable. They see pedagogical flexibility, teacher control, and accessibility as the key issues in adoption of technology in the classroom.

In the 1980s studies began on media comparisons concerned with developmental cognitive processes and their relationship to specific media attributes. Aptitude-treatment research was focused on which attributes were most effective. New theories of active TV viewing were brought forth, arguing against the previous notion of passive television viewing. Specific attributes of viewers in connection with TV were also investigated (Saettler, 1990).

PROGRAMMED INSTRUCTION AND COMPUTER-ASSISTED INSTRUCTION MOVEMENTS

As early as the 1950s, educational technology approaches began to incorporate the computer through the programmed instruction movement. This movement revived individualizing instruction notions based on behaviorism. However, by the late 1960s the programmed instruction movement was in decline. Another important computer-based movement was computer-aided instruction (CAI), first used in the 1950s. Much of the early work developing this approach was done at International Business Machines (IBM). CAI growth occurred in the mid-1960s, but faded quickly by the late 1960s. The typical CAI program included drill-and-practice and tutorial with a strong degree of author (or software designer) rather than learner control. Other computer-based educational technology movements include intelligent computer-aided instruction (ICAI) and intelligent tutoring systems (ITS), both developed from cognitive science approaches to educational technology (Saettler, 1990). In the next chapter, the discussion of educational technology uses of the computer, particularly as they relate to specific learning theories, is continued.

INTERNATIONAL DISTANCE LEARNING MOVEMENTS

On the international level, the University of London conducted examinations and began offering degrees to external students in 1836. This paved the way for the growth of private correspondence colleges that prepared students for the University of London examinations and enabled them to study independently without enrolling as traditional students in the university. A British Extension Movement emerged in the 1870s, and by 1884 its leaders pressed for a part-time, non-resident institution operating with academic credits. More recently, the international Open University Movement has been a leading force in distance education. According to Rumble and Harry (1982), the foundation of the international Open University Movement in the 1970s stemmed from a concern for greater equality of opportunity in access to higher education.

The printed text has been the principal teaching medium in most Open University courses, although this is changing somewhat with the increased use of the Internet and computer. Rumble and Harry (1982) claim that one political aspect of the development of open universities is that in some countries (Free University of Iran, Open University of China), distance learning courses have been seen as a way of keeping students off campuses for fear that the students will be politicized. Nevertheless, the overall political motivation to develop such institutions, according to the research literature, has been a populist desire to provide general access to higher education.

CURRENT LITERATURE ON THE ADMINISTRATION OF DISTANCE LEARNING INNOVATION IN HIGHER EDUCATION

In reviewing the relevant literature on the administration of distance learning, the expansive body of research on the nature of change in organizations and in educational institutions in particular was encountered repeatedly. Inasmuch as implementing distance learning, according to some advocates, requires administrative change, it is important here to briefly review this literature. The literature is divided primarily into focusing on the nature of innovation and change, the special characteristics of academic change, change in K–12 environments, and corporate change.

What can we learn about distance learning implementation in the literature on change and innovation? Miles (1964) defines innovations as willful and planned-for change placed within a social environment. For him, innovations are always operating in relation to a given social system and are rejected, modified, accepted, and maintained by forces in the system. Rogers (1962) defines innovation simply as an idea perceived as new. The five characteristics of innovations, according to him, are advantage, compatibility, complexity, divisibility, and communicability. Advantage is the merit of the innovation over current practices. Compatibility is the degree to which an innovation is consistent with existing values and past experiences of the adopters. The complexity of an innovation as perceived by members of a social system adversely affects its rate of adoption. Divisibility is the degree to which an innovation may be tried on a limited basis. Communicability is the ease by which the innovation can be described. Distance learning has potential problems in each of these areas. In contrast to Rogers, James Burke argues that change just happens and almost always comes as a surprise (Abbott, 1999). Burke describes a theory of change based on the critical importance of communication systems.

Miles (1964) claims that academic institutions change more slowly than any others. Indeed, Mort (1964) argues that there is typically a lag of 50 years between recognition of the need for change and the introduction of an innovation in education. While today this estimate of the slowness of academic change is clearly an exaggeration, the general characterization of higher education in comparison to other types of organizations has validity. Why does innovation in education take so long? The literature on innovation in education points to a lack of change agents and economic incentives (Eicholz & Rogers, 1964; Mort, 1964). Additionally, innovation is connected directly with an external orientation of change leaders and organizations as a whole (Eicholz & Rogers, 1964). The greater the external awareness, the more likely individuals and groups will behave in an innovative fashion. The literature suggests that educational institutions typically do not have this external focus.

Sarason (1996), one of the leading scholars on school change, particularly at the K–12 level, argues that organizational studies of schools are borrowed largely from industry and have not often understood the vast differences between the two cultures. Sarason sees the view of the school as an autonomous system as the source of the misguided belief that schools are vehicles for social change. They are far from autonomous, and their power is unequally distributed—consequently, change in schools requires an alteration in the power structure. As we saw others have claimed, Sarason argues that there needs to be strong external forces pushing change. Public dissatisfaction with schools will continue to be the decisive force in bringing change to education. Sarason sees the current dissatisfaction as not new, but as historical in its intensity. Although he was writing primarily about K–12 education, Sarason's ideas about change and external forces are relevant to current discussions about distance learning in higher education. Are external forces pressing for change through distance learning?

There is a large body of research on educational reform specifically in relationship to higher education (Boyer, 1984; Hefferlin, 1969; Martin, 1968; Miller, 1998). Boyer (1984) describes what he terms "experimental education," traced to the 1950s with institutions such as Reed College, Antioch, Monteith, Goddard, and Bennington. It is his argument that since then experimentation in higher education has become a norm. In contrast to Boyer, Miller (1998) claims that universities are complex bureaucracies that are inherently resistant to structural change of any kind. Martin (1968) argues that the challenge for higher education is to find ways to listen to outside criticism without sacrificing independence. His solution is to increase structural diversity and create pockets of experimentation within large universities.

One of the general observations about change in the university is that it is a complex and nonlinear process (Johnson, 1999). Johnson advised that before introducing formal policies and approaches, there is a need for informal groups and individuals interested in the particular change effort to work together. Strong leadership does not imply a top-down approach, but rather an environment where bottom-up action is encouraged in order to meet shared goals. Johnson recommends that program evaluation be used to ensure that resources are used effectively and that outcomes are worthwhile.

Many in the research literature focus on organizational culture and change. Levine (1999) argues that many attempts at change in education over the past 30 years have failed because the focus was on change itself and not on the institutions' needs and outcomes as reflected by their particular culture. The change effort was for its own sake, and involved mandated approaches that were not effective. According to Levine, most educational cultures constrain change, thus requiring slow and strategically integrated efforts. The reshaping of values and beliefs, as well as the changing of orga-nizational norms, needs to occur through the involvement of stakeholders.

The research literature about change in higher education often discusses the dynamics of groups (Schmuck & Runkel, 1994). Schmuck and Runkel argue that change is made from within an organization, not through out-side experts. While educational institutions are attuned to individual de-velopment, they are notoriously weak in nurturing their own social subsystems for organizational development and find cooperation difficult. Schmuck and Runkel hold that the manner of work should change, and that demands among individuals working together also need to change. Thus groups are targeted in their model. However, they caution that it is common for factions within colleges to have different educational goals. Conflict arises when particular educational goals are perceived as being mutually exclusive or when parties fight for resources.

Fullan (1993) points out that the change process is complex, and thus one must focus on the process. He argues that the education system is fun-damentally conservative and that the status quo is protected by teacher training, school organization, and political decision makers. Attempts at change in this kind of environment lead to defensiveness, superficiality, and small successes. Fullan claims that change often fails because it does not address fundamental instructional reform. In the context of distance learning, one needs to ask, does technology provide this attempt at funda-mental instructional reform?

CHANGE AND TECHNOLOGY

In recent years, a growing body of literature has addressed how technology is incorporated in educational institutions. The research literature can be broken into the following categories: educational reform, administrative values, context and culture, constructivist orientations, and critical per-spectives. The literature on organizational issues and the use of distance learning is limited but growing. In America, community colleges have demonstrated the greatest use of and commitment to the application of dis-tance education technologies (Dillon & Cintron, 1997), and consequently the literature on community colleges is the largest.

Katz and Rudy (1999) point to the importance of understanding the context in which technology investments are being made. They suggest that institutions should ask how they can advance their institutional goals through an investment in technology. To effect change, a clear sense of purpose or mission is required. On a cultural level, Katz and Rudy suggest that it is important to understand how institutions organized around shared governance make decisions about uses of technology and modes of learning. Taylor and Eustis (1999) argue that universities have been quick to adopt technology, but slow to adjust organizational structures to take advantage of the resulting potential to increase productivity. They see technology as a way to restructure an organization. Consistently, the literature discusses the need for distance learning to be in line with institutional values (Parisot, 1997; Lape & Hart, 1997). Also, repeatedly there is mention of the need for distance learning to have value beyond the use of technology for its own sake.

Means (1994) argues that school reform is undertaken without consideration of the facilitating role that technology might play. In and of itself, technology contains neither pedagogical philosophy nor content bias. Means points out that technology should not be viewed as an end in itself, but related to increased student involvement with complex tasks and new organizational structures. He sees technology used for four broad purposes: to tutor, to explore, as tools, and to communicate. Means holds that because technology supports communication, it is highly compatible with project-based, constructivist approaches. Instead, however, drill-and-practice software has found acceptance in schools because it fits into existing educational structures.

Sheingold and Frederiksen (1994) argue that the link between assessment and reform cannot be made without considerable use of technology. Technologies are critically important in education reform because they increase student work that can be used in assessment and provide a medium for conversations about values and standards for student performance. In a similar vein, Herman (1994) argues that technology is often seen as a failure in education reform. However, the methodologies for assessing effectiveness may be faulty. Comparison studies in the use of technology have trouble finding truly comparable groups. Herman points out that one cannot separate technology from the quality of instruction and curriculum where it is embedded. Implementation data must be collected to see if the technology is implemented as planned. The use of technology for teaching raises fundamental questions about populations served, methods of teaching, priorities for funding, and goals and purpose of the university. Thus, Bates (2000a; 2000b) argues that technology plans should be subordinate to overall educational goals. The use of technology needs to be embedded in an overall teaching plan.

The literature also contains many criticisms and questions about distance learning from an administrative point of view. Chambers (1999) claims that it may produce effective workers, but questions whether it produces creative and critical thinkers. Weaknesses of distance learning pointed out in the literature include a mechanistic approach to management resulting in an inflexibility to respond to change. Additionally, the separation between educational provider and student works against informal forms of feedback. Furthermore, Powell, McGuire, and Crawford (1999) argue that institutions often get locked into high-cost technological ventures, thus taking their focus off pedagogical issues. More generally, the traditional community of scholars in higher education is often alienated by Taylorist approaches to higher education management. By uncritically adopting high technology, universities may only achieve both high costs and ineffective teaching. Finally, Tait (1999) argues that lifelong learning has come to have more of an economic than an academic emphasis in keeping individuals employable and businesses competitive.

CORPORATE CHANGE

The literature on corporate change and the use of distance learning shows concerns similar to those discovered in the literature on academic change, but with a stronger emphasis on the economic aspects. Chute, Thompson, and Hancock (1999) argue that motivation for change in organizations has to do with a realization that the cost of not changing is greater than that of changing. Once the change is made, it is seen as important to incorporate it in the organization. Middle level and lower level buy-in with technology change is crucial. They argue that insufficient planning and poor project management are typical reasons for the failure to implement distance learning in business settings. Business, information systems, and training functions are needed for implementation. In business settings, travel cost savings are one big benefit of distance learning. Another economic issue for businesses using distance learning is the productivity benefit from distance learning training.

According to Oblinger and Katz (2000), one of the reasons for moving to e-business models is that such a move allows, or even forces, organizations to innovate. Peter Senge (2000) argues that universities have become the preeminent knowing institutions, yet the world of business is increasingly moving toward learning institutions. He foresees innovation processes within universities in the future centering on clusters of faculty and spreading through informal rather than formal organizational channels.

ROLE OF THE FACULTY

In looking at the change process, the research literature often points to the role of faculty, generally focusing on its members' resistance to the use of technology. Many in the literature comment on how the faculty tend to be teacher-centered and thus view technology as an aid to support teacher-centered strategies rather than as a vehicle for changing approaches to teaching. Looked at positively, Wallhaus (2000) claims that faculty who use technology effectively will find it easier and more compelling to collaborate with outside providers, colleagues, and other units within the university through distance learning. Nevertheless, the change brought about by the use of technology gives rise to important questions about faculty, including, most importantly, compensation. What compensation rates are used? What formula for load credit is used? How are faculty paid or provided compensatory time for course development? Who owns course materials and other intellectual property? How is faculty productivity measured without contact time? Wallhaus sees one possible solution in competency-based measures.

Anandam (1998) argues that administrators need to focus on mainstream faculty, not just champions of change in an implementation process. The literature shows that often those faculty who use distance education feel confident about the methodology and request its use. Conversely, educators with little awareness or understanding about distance learning tend to question its viability and effectiveness. Research indicates that support or resistance of department chairs and division directors comprises an important variable in instructional change. One study found that the greatest skepticism about academic performance of distance learning students occurred at the dean level (Lape & Hart, 1997).

Lucas and associates (2000) argue that it is predictable that resistance occurs when faculty, accustomed to autonomy, are asked to participate in change initiatives, because they fear they will be distracted from their own professional agendas. Kovalchick (1999) argues that faculty resistance to new technology is a rational reaction to a lack of formal training in learning and instructional theory. She sees a natural tension in the implementation process between the adoption of new technological materials versus new teaching methods. Angelo (2000) claims that change efforts often fail because they are implemented piecemeal, and without an understanding of the specific circumstances and strategies that are likely to promote them with the faculty.

LEADING ADMINISTRATIVE MODELS

The University of Phoenix and the British Open University represent two of the most influential new models in higher education. While the University of Phoenix delivers the majority of its courses through face-to-face contact, it also has a large distance learning program. Many of the innovations that the University of Phoenix has developed in its central programs, such as one-course terms, cohorts, development of courses through expert teams, and the almost exclusive use of part-time faculty, are present in the distance learning courses as well. Baker (1999) from the University of Phoenix argues for the need for clear interactional guidelines, accessible administrative systems, technical flexibility, faculty training, curriculum consistency, and advance student preparation for successful online degree implementation. One can see that the approach of the University of Phoenix to its online courses is consistent with its learner-centered, student service, materials-based overall approach.

As one of the most successful nontraditional institutions with a research emphasis, the British Open University has become a major contributor to both administrative and pedagogical literature in the field. Eisenstadt and Vincent (2000) claim that the success of the Open University is based on high-quality content, student support, effective logistics, and a strong research base. In the British Open University, instructors are known as tutors. Each student studies at home using teaching materials delivered primarily by mail that employ a variety of media. For each course, the student is allocated a local tutor who teaches via correspondence and helps with queries related to the academic materials. The tutor is normally contacted by telephone, mail, and increasingly by email. Students may also attend local, face-to-face tutorials run by their tutors, and they may choose to form self-help groups with other students (Petre, Carswell, Price & Thomas, 2000).

According to Petre, Carswell, Price, and Thomas (2000), the mainstay of teaching at the British Open University is the tutor-marked assignment (TMA). Tutor notes, including a marking scheme, are provided to the tutor in order to ensure assessment quality, and marked assignments are monitored regularly for consistency and quality. Discussion sessions known as tutorials are crucial in establishing student networks and self-help groups. Tutorials provide alternative perspectives and explanations, structure, and incentives, and facilitate learning from other students. Asynchronous group work is organized by student choice of projects.

The British Open University emphasizes the problem-based learning format intended to challenge learners to discover what they know and apply that knowledge to finding methods of solving problems. Additionally, the problem-based learning format attempts to give students increasingly difficult problems supported by helpful hints and Socratic-style interaction (Chambers, 1999). The terms "flexible learning" and "flexible delivery" employed by the British Open University show an intention to increase learners' access to and control over particular teaching and learning environments (Kirkpatrick & Jakupec, 1999). Flexibility often requires more sophisticated activities and technologies, technical backup, and support structures. The British Open University's open and distant learning (ODL) differs from correspondence instruction in the use of multiple media as well as the use of small-group and individual student support and teaching (Mills, 1999). The emphasis on tutor and individual student interaction is meant to compensate for the lack of face-to-face lectures at the British Open University. Mills notes that the tutorial system of Oxford and Cambridge was combined with ODL so that individual students receive detailed written reactions to their work. This tutorial system has been a key element of the Open University administrative and pedagogical approach.

In addition to the tutorial model, the British Open University focuses on media-rich experiences that involve video, simulation models, and sophisticated animations (Eisenstadt & Vincent, 2000). This media-rich approach derives from what Eisenstadt and Vincent claim is a constructivist approach at the British Open University, based on what they describe as a belief in the importance of learners creating their own content. This kind of customization attempt, while reaching very large audiences, is what is remarkable and different in this so-called mega-university. The British Open University prefers to describe its method as "supported open learning" rather than "distance learning" to emphasize the tutorial and support structure for individualized learning. Eisenstadt and Vincent do not believe in delivering courses entirely on the World Wide Web, a view that at least partly reflects the general British Open University attitude toward online courses. Furthermore, rather than dismissing traditional media such as television, they appreciate the use of traditional media in educational environments.

John Daniel, the vice-chancellor of the British Open University, is probably its most articulate representative. According to Daniel (2000), distance education has two very different traditions: individual learning and group teaching. He sees distance learning's advantage in its ability to offer individual learning opportunities, which is what the British Open University does. Group teaching leads to the loss of opportunity to address the needs of access, cost, and flexibility. Daniel wonders why American higher education in particular focuses on group learning. He concludes that this emphasis on group classroom learning results from American higher education valuing teaching over learning. For instance, with the seeming American preoccupation with videoconferencing, the interactive value goes sharply down as student numbers go up, while this is not the case in online environments, according to Daniel. Daniel claims that the Holy

Grail of education has been found in distance education because we now have a delivery system where more students create better, not worse, education experiences.

LEADING GOVERNMENT-SPONSORED MODELS: CALIFORNIA VIRTUAL UNIVERSITY (CVU) AND THE WESTERN GOVERNORS UNIVERSITY (WGU)

In the United States, two recent government efforts at instituting and encouraging distance learning are relevant to the discussion of administrative practices. While the California Virtual University is now essentially defunct and the Western Governors University has been slow to meet enrollment expectations, they offer insight as examples of approaches to distance learning administration.

The official origin of the Western Governors University was a memorandum of understanding that followed the positive reception of a report from a design team. Ten states initially participated, including Arizona, Colorado, Idaho, Nebraska, New Mexico, North Dakota, Oregon, Utah, Washington, and Wyoming. The memorandum cited specific needs that it wanted to address, including access, affordability, and certification. In the subsequent Resolution 96–002, signed June 24, 1996, the Western Governors Association also agreed to support collaboration with businesses, between universities, and among states on financial aid issues. The governors charged a design team with creating a design plan for a virtual university describing how such an entity could be developed and financed. The primary elements of the mission of this entity, adapted from "From Vision to Reality," were identified as expanding access, formal recognition of skills and knowledge, shifting the focus of education to competence from "seat time," and new approaches to teaching and assessment. The strategic implementation was based on a market orientation that is learner-centered, accredited, competency-based, regional, and quickly initiated. In their prospectus, the design team identified their basic approach as creating broader markets for existing educational services, fostering the development of new products where unmet needs are identified, utilizing market mechanisms, and removing barriers to interstate flows of educational activities. Further, they identified the role of the WGU as providing the means for assessing an individual's competence, acting as a vehicle for identifying providers of educational programs, and providing support services.

Most important, the prospectus advocated the creation of regional centers franchised by the WGU as points of access for services. These regional centers would not necessarily be existing educational institutions. Organizations were to apply to become regional centers, and for-profit businesses were not to be excluded. The WGU has contracted with providers of educational materials and assessment instruments. Essentially, the WGU is promoting the creation of both a consortium and a new educational institution which is separately accredited. The role of the WGU is to provide centralized governance, policy guidance, and quality control. Currently, the WGU is still in an early phase of development after receiving low enrollments for its initial offerings. As of late 2001, it was attempting to expand its operation and seek additional higher education partners.

In 1989 the California legislature approved Senate Bill 1202, which directed the California Post-Secondary Education Commission (CPEC) to develop a state policy on distance learning. The resulting report, "State Policy on Technology for Distance Learning," suggested a policy emphasizing equity, quality, diversity, efficiency, and accountability. However, largely because of the extreme funding cutbacks in the early nineties, the distance learning plans could not be implemented by the legislature.

In 1996 the economy began to turn around in California and the distance learning initiatives were picked up again. With CPEC projecting an additional 450,000 college-age students over the next decade in California, the legislature looked at technology as a partial solution. CPEC subsequently wrote two reports, "Moving Forward: A Preliminary Discussion of Technology and Transformation in California Higher Education" (1996) and "Coming of Information Age in California Higher Education" (1997), attempting to address the need for an overall statewide approach to technology in education.

Executive Order W-153–97 established the California Virtual University Design Team with the charge of recommending a blueprint to meet somewhat vague needs. In the 1998–99 budget, Governor Pete Wilson requested a total of $14 million to encourage distance learning, with $6.1 million specifically earmarked for CVU. Wilson's plans included $1 million each for the University of California (UC) and California State University (CSU) to develop online courses, and $3.9 million for the California Community Colleges (Coleman, 1998).

Assembly Bill 2431 was introduced on February 20, 1998, paving the way for creating standards of distance learning practice in California and establishing the Matching Grant Program to assist California institutions in the development of distance learning courses. The text of the bill states, "Distance education shall be utilized by the state to achieve its goals for education, equity, quality, choice, efficiency, and accountability" (State of California, 1998).

The Western Governors Association and California Virtual University efforts are similar, most importantly in their brokering management approach. As an article in the *Chronicle of Higher Education* reveals, the WGU sees itself to some degree as an enormous course broker: "Governor Leavitt [of Utah], in fact, likens the new institution to 'a kind of New York Stock Exchange of Technology-delivered courses'" (Blumenstyk, 1998b). Although the WGU originally sought separate accreditation, it remains to be seen if it will develop its own courses to any extent. In this way, the WGU and CVU avoided obvious competitive battles with existing higher education institutions through a brokering mandate. However, this strategy also severely limits the real impact and value of both of these institutions.

The Western Governors Association and the state of California both are encouraging participation from private industry, which has left them open to criticism from those who insist on a traditional separation of the university from business. Furthermore, the objectives of both organizations are similar in their declared aims of meeting changing student and business needs, providing access for the increased student population, and increasing the quality of distance format courses.

While there are obvious similarities between the Western Governors Association and the state of California's efforts at creating distance learning institutions, there are important differences. Overall, the Western Governors Association effort was both more ambitious and further developed. This necessarily gave California's effort less impact because students could not complete a degree through the virtual university, only through individual institutions. Furthermore, the WGU is a multistate effort, while the CVU was exclusively based within California. This makes the WGU's implementation much more difficult—and ultimately more important if it is successful—because it will have addressed the serious financial, funding, and transferability issues that go along with interstate cooperation. In addition, the WGU has a training orientation in its initial curriculum and has decided to focus on A.A. degrees at the outset, rather than bachelor's degrees. Undoubtedly this decision is a result of the influence of its corporate advisors. It is difficult to tell if this emphasis on training and on A.A. degrees is a strategic marketing decision or an academic one.

Training versus a traditional education model is clearly a preoccupation for the WGU. Conversely, California's effort concentrated to a great extent on building a technological infrastructure for its three enormous higher education systems. While the Virtual University catalogue in California listed independent institutions, they were left out of the infrastructure plans. As a consortium of various state and private institutions, the WGU has more difficulty addressing infrastructure issues by legislative measures.

Perhaps the single most important difference between the two government efforts concerns the issue of competency-based credit. While the state of California is experimenting with competency-based credit at CSU Monterey, this was not part of the Virtual University planning. For the WGU, competency-based credit is integral to the overall theory and implementation of its distance learning. The widespread implementation of competency-based credit would in fact be revolutionary in its effect on higher education administration.

DISTANCE LEARNING BEST PRACTICES DEBATE

In evaluating and understanding administrative practices in higher education in connection with distance learning, it is useful to look at the various recent attempts to construct a best practices model. In response to these concerns about the administration of distance learning programs in higher education, a number of organizations have adopted guidelines. Those of the American Council on Education (ACE) are titled "Guiding Principles for Distance Learning in a Learning Society." The Accrediting Commission for Community and Junior Colleges, Western Association of Schools and Colleges (1999) issued its 1999 *Distance Education Handbook* focusing on the issues of motivation, partnerships, mission, faculty, students, special needs students, library access, student outcomes, planning, facilities, marketing, and intellectual property rights. The Western Interstate Commission for Higher Education's (WICHE) "Good Practices in Distance Education" (1997) has been one of the most influential attempts to date at providing guidelines for distance learning and offers a good framework for examining distance learning implementation. This document is a product of a three-year project supported by the Fund for the Improvement of Post-Secondary Education (FIPSE) called Balancing Quality and Access: Reducing State Policy Barriers to Electronically Delivered Higher Education Programs. The principles have been endorsed by a number of higher education associations and accrediting agencies. The preamble to the principles claims that in recognizing the changing context for learning, the authors tried not to tie them to traditional campus structures. Nevertheless, the guidelines seem to be very traditional in focusing on accreditation bodies, curriculum, faculty oversight, resources, student services, and assessment. It is particularly telling that rather than addressing pedagogical questions, the principles call for "appropriate" faculty and student interaction.

Probably the most important aspect of WICHE's standards in relationship to implementation is the call for new distance learning programs to be "consistent with the institution's role and mission" (Western Interstate

Commission on Higher Education, 1997, p. 7). While this is a standard criterion considered by accrediting agencies in looking at new program development, it has special meaning in regard to distance learning. Since distance learning has been identified with revenue generation (see Chapter 4) and raises questions about teaching methods, traditional university roles and missions often are a problematic fit. While WICHE's standards are useful as a beginning step for many institutions, a more detailed understanding of how they are applied in specific settings is necessary. To this end, WICHE includes short case studies and examples of how various institutions are practicing distance learning in an effective manner.

The most important standards under development for distance learning practice are those of the regional accrediting agencies. Regional accrediting agencies are recognized by the U.S. Department of Education as entities whose accreditation enables their member institutions to seek eligibility to participate in Title IV programs. Pressure from various sources seems to be pushing the accrediting agencies to focus on the issue of quality in distance education through revising standards. The purpose of this new effort is to assure that quality standards are upheld during a period of rapid growth in the use of technology in higher education. In September 2000, the eight regional accrediting commissions issued a draft "Statement of the Regional Accrediting Commissions on the Evaluation of Electronically Offered Degree and Certificate Programs" (Council of Regional Accrediting Commissions, 2000b). In this document, the Council of Regional Accrediting Commissions (C-RAC) explains that it contracted with the Western Cooperative for Educational Telecommunications (WCET) to create "Guidelines for the Evaluation of Electronically Offered Degree and Certificate Programs" (Council of Regional Accrediting Commissions, 2000a). The regional accrediting commissions recognize the problem of the whole notion of regional accreditation when educational programs are no longer tied to location in distance learning programs. Thus, they felt a need to outline joint standards. The guidelines are not a departure from regional standards, but rather an attempt to apply traditional standards of institutional quality to new forms of learning. Most important, the guidelines specifically require that all "big decisions" are to be made by faculty.

CONCLUSION

The historical, educational change, and best practices literature on distance learning reveal the following major points relevant to the discussion about distance learning administration in higher education: (1) historically, distance learning courses in American higher education did not try to replace traditional higher education; (2) distance learning courses were aimed at nontraditional student populations who did not have access to higher education; (3) distance learning courses grew out of the University Extension Movement, not the university proper; (4) because of a history of serving different populations in different ways, academic quality, standards, and pedagogical techniques have been applied unsystematically; (5) the process of change and innovation in higher education is generally difficult; (6) faculty play a key role in change models; (7) prominent models of distance learning administration radically alter traditional higher education organizational structure; and (8) attempts to construct best practices for distance learning rely heavily on traditional notions of academic quality.

First, while distance learning instruction was seen as a way of either augmenting the traditional university education (as in the case of the Correspondence University) or leading students into traditional degree programs (University of Chicago and Chautauqua), it was never seen as a replacement. Since correspondence instruction was aimed at nontraditional university populations and because it did not intend to replace traditional instruction, it did not spark resistance from the faculty. Consequently, it will be important to see in this book whether or not distance learning efforts are housed in university extension units, as has often been the case historically, or if they reside in academic departments.

Second, the origin of distance learning courses in America reflects many needs that still must be addressed today: geographic access, flexible scheduling, access by specific populations, and expanded curriculum offerings. While the enormous growth of higher education institutions, particularly community colleges, in the latter half of the twentieth century has provided greater geographic access, this is still an issue for those living in rural areas. More important, convenient scheduling has become increasingly crucial as the demands of work and family have shortened the time available for study, especially for adults. While there have been great gains in access to higher education for particular populations, especially women, over the past century, students with economic challenges by no means have equal access. The number and variety of courses in universities have certainly exploded in the last century, but not all subjects or all faculty members are equally available. Consequently, all of the factors that led to the development of correspondence courses (geographic distance; demands of work and military service; prejudicial lack of access for women, minorities, and the handicapped; religious convictions; and limitations of the curriculum) are still relevant today to some degree. Consequently, it is interesting to see in this book how these factors have led to motivations for implementing distance learning in the respondents.

Third, the origin of correspondence instruction in the Chautauqua and the University Extension movements reveals an important connection between distance learning and continuing education. We can see from the short history described above that the rise of the adult learner in higher education developed hand-in-hand with the popularity of correspondence courses. The Chautauqua Movement and subsequently the University of Chicago in many ways form the historical roots of many of the innovations in higher education, including university extension, summer sessions, university presses, and correspondence courses. The history of the University of Chicago shows that correspondence courses were structured from the beginning as a part of university extension. While the general idea of university extension was widely imitated, rarely did such divisions hold as prominent a place in university structure as at the University of Chicago. As courses offered through extension divisions in universities, the correspondence courses have been tolerated. In contrast, at the University of Chicago, regular faculty were involved to a great degree and saw home study as an opportunity for additional income. The Home Study Program was discontinued because of increased competition from publicly supported institutions, not because of faculty objections over academic quality.

Fourth, because of a history of serving different populations in different ways through distance learning instruction, academic quality, standards, and pedagogical approaches have been unsystematically applied. There is very little literature about the history of pedagogical issues in connection with distance learning from correspondence courses to educational television and online courses (this is addressed further in the next chapter). The methods of distance learning instruction have varied greatly, from partial residency programs at Chautauqua, to the use of recordings in language courses, to the complex multimedia used in courses offered at present. This anarchy in teaching method reflects the diverse course providers and the wide range of student needs. Although the development of standards through the Home Study Council and various accrediting agencies has been adopted over the years, they do not replace real research on the pedagogy of distance learning. An important aim of this book is to evaluate the academic quality of distance learning through administrative practices such as faculty oversight, course development, assessment of student learning, and pedagogical sophistication.

Fifth, change and innovation in higher education are generally difficult to accomplish. Universities are very complex organizations with power structures often broadly distributed, and consequently are by their very nature slow moving. Since distance learning may involve both administrative and pedagogical innovation, it is natural that it would meet resistance and be slowly implemented.

Sixth, the possible effect on faculty in terms of compensation rates and employment status is resulting in a further slowing of the implementation process. Issues such as the increased use of part-time faculty and the possible loss by faculty of intellectual property make distance learning particularly susceptible to controversy (this is addressed in detail in Chapter 4). Nevertheless, we can see from the research literature that the pressures to implement distance learning are great, and in some cases stronger than the resistance.

Seventh, prominent models of distance learning administration radically alter traditional higher education organizational structure. Although the University of Phoenix is not primarily a distance learning institution, it has come to symbolize in many people's minds the administrative changes brought about by distance learning. The almost exclusive use of part-time faculty, the reliance on courses developed by teams, and the lack of administrative control by faculty, along with the different pedagogical approaches, are all radical changes to traditional higher education practice. The British Open University model presents in some ways an even more radical shift in organizational structure because it attempts to be a high-quality research institution while giving full access to its curriculum through innovative teaching methods. Its focus on teaching material development or "knowledge media," as well as facilitating learning through tutors, points higher education in a very different direction for the future. Government models such as the Western Governors University challenge traditional measures of seat time by focusing on competency outcomes. A competency-based system of granting credit could severely alter higher education in America.

Eighth, attempts to construct best practices for distance learning rely heavily on traditional measures of academic quality. The focus of the various professional organizations and accrediting bodies on faculty oversight and other traditional standards reveals an attempt to retain traditional approaches to higher education while simultaneously trying to accommodate radical change.

One can see from the review of the literature on distance learning administrative practices in higher education in this chapter that it is a complex subject, with a long and often contentious history. In the interviews presented later we will see this complexity confirmed, particularly as the respondents describe the history of distance learning at their individual institutions. The quantitative data returned from the survey will reveal important information on current administrative practices, not only on motivation for the use of distance learning, but also on key budgetary, academic, and faculty issues. In the next chapter we turn to a review of the growing literature on distance learning pedagogical theory to better understand in the end how administrative practices connect to teaching/learning approaches.

CHAPTER

Review of Distance Learning Pedagogical Literature

How are institutional motivations affecting the manner in which pedagogical issues are addressed?

This chapter examines the current state of research on the pedagogy of distance learning. This area is important for this study because in examining the implications of different institutional motives for the use of distance learning, the resulting effects on approaches to teaching and learning are central. In order to judge properly the sophistication of an institutional approach to distance learning pedagogy, a general understanding of research in this field is needed. Indicators of how institutional motivation to adopt distance learning affects pedagogical approaches are seen in the data on length and expense of course development, use of multiple technologies and media, and prevalence of more advanced teaching approaches, including group projects, simulations, and the attention to interaction issues, computer interface design, and navigational strategies.

HISTORY

The history of educational technology connected to pedagogy shows a pattern of exaggerated promise at the new technology's introduction, generally followed by disappointment. Thomas Edison predicted in 1913 that books would be replaced by motion pictures (Cuban, 1986). In 1940 George F. Zook, in his American Council on Education report, described film as "the most revolutionary instrument introduced in education since the printing press" (Hoban, 1942, p. 16). While film came into wide use in educational environments during World War II when the military needed a device to speed up the training of masses of soldiers with various skill levels and education, it never gained acceptance in higher education in the same way (Hoban, 1942). After these early periods of great promise, the history of the use of technology in education largely reflects resistance to change and disappointment.

The literature on the use of film and TV in educational environments is striking in that one finds much written and published in the period of the 1930s–1950s, and then very little afterwards. Research in the uses of film in education remained almost at a standstill during the late fifties and sixties. In the seventies and eighties, a few authors focused on how to use films to teach creatively as an augmentation and resource in the classroom (Schillaci & Culkin, 1970; Worth, 1981), while others argued about the educational value of film and television, especially *Sesame Street* (Goldman & Burnett, 1971; Cook, et al., 1975). Instructional television and videotape courses became commonplace in the 1960s and were much publicized as being the wave of the future. Although they have certainly played a role, their acceptance has been much less widespread than anticipated. Overall, surprisingly little has been written about the uses of film and television in education.

With the introduction of the personal computer, large claims were once again made for educational applications. The programmed learning movement, or auto-instructional movement, began with the introduction of computers and early on emphasized B. F. Skinner's model of operant conditioning, response mode, error rate, and reinforcement (DeCecco, 1964). Later, computer-aided instruction (CAI) and then intelligent computer-aided instruction (ICAI) developed, seeking to utilize artificial intelligence capabilities. ICAI in particular hoped to use developing artificial intelligence software programs to react to student responses in a more lifelike fashion (Frasson & Gauthier, 1990). However, neither of these movements had much success in either K–12 or higher education. In looking at the history of educational technology, one can see that one of the problems has been the lack of clear pedagogical approaches to the use of various technologies.

BEHAVIORISM VERSUS CONSTRUCTIVISM

Not surprisingly, the pedagogical approach to the use of technology in the classroom has swung back and forth between behaviorists and constructivists, both schools in many cases also exaggerating technology's promise. For constructivists, computers may finally provide the means by which the very labor-intensive educational philosophy of John Dewey may be put into practice. On the other side of the fence, behaviorists have long held sway in the field of computer-based training (CBT), with the tireless repetition and utilization of clear behavioral learning objectives being key elements of these training programs.

In *The Technology of Teaching*, Skinner (1964) argued that the use of technology in teaching can increase learned behavior by organizing learning objectives, increasing the frequency of positive reinforcement, customizing the learning experience, and freeing teachers from repetitive teaching. The teaching machine is essentially a reinforcer—Skinner saw the key advantage of teaching machines in that the user receives immediate feedback from the machine. He promoted the notion of teaching machine as tutor in pacing students through appropriate level material, and through prompting, hinting, and suggesting ways students can arrive at correct answers. In addition, Skinner pointed to the advantages of teaching machines beyond issues of behavior modification in that they make possible improvements in class management, asynchronous learning, and customization.

As behaviorism declined more generally in other fields in the late 1950s, it became more important to educational technology. Behaviorist approaches led to step-by-step units of instruction focused on measurable learning products. Cognitive approaches, in contrast to behaviorism, focus on internal process and knowing rather than responding. It wasn't until the early 1980s that the cognitive model began to replace the behaviorist approaches to educational technology. Consequently, issues of learners organizing, processing, and storing information became important. Jean Piaget and his model of cognition provided a new guide and approach to problems of instructional design. His scheme is one of adaptation where learners strive to achieve equilibrium or stability between themselves and their environment. Equilibrium depends on two processes: assimilation and accommodation. Instructional designers use Piaget's model to synchronize instruction with individual development.

Overall, the constructivist framework emphasizes assisting students in constructing their own knowledge through the use of computers. An active learner elaborates upon and interprets the information presented in an instructional program. A constructivist approach need not only consist of the discovery learning type, but can also focus on more direct instruction as long as the stress is ongoing beyond the information given. For constructivists, context is an integral part of meaning. Consequently, constructivists propose working with concepts in complicated computer environments that lead students to see complex interrelationships. The goal is to create a computer environment where tasks take on meaning in a larger context.

One of the most high-profile figures in the computer-enabling learning field over the years has been Seymour Papert from MIT, who has a constructivist orientation. Papert (1993) sees value not only in having students use computer applications, but in having them learn how to write programming languages. Papert's computer language, Logo, is designed to give children an opportunity to create simple computer programs by moving a turtle in different directions on the computer screen. He emphasizes a constructivist approach and puts forward the notion of "mathetics," by which he means the art of learning. Papert believes that the use of simple programming languages allows students to learn by a process he terms "bricolage." Bricolage is a style of organizing thinking that is done improvisationally rather than planned in advance. By placing themselves inside the symbolic universe of computer programming and trying to move about, the students are put in close relationship to their problem. This basic principle of using a computer as a tool to visualize the thinking process is discussed consistently in the literature, usually in arguments promoting the advantages of metacognition, or learning how to learn.

Critics of Skinner's position on technology point to his overemphasis on changed behavior as learning. His methods are useful for repetitive learning, but they don't begin to get at the real potential of a teaching machine. According to critics, Skinner misses the real value of educational technology because he focused on reinforcement of behavior rather than seeing the potential of a new learning tool that can assist deeper and more creative thinking.

Critics of the application of constructivism to educational technology raise questions about the effectiveness of constructivist instruction when it tries to cover too much material, the lack of concern with the skill level of students, and the reliability of evaluation methods. Furthermore, contrary to the constructivists, some argue that different organizations of knowledge are required to promote different learning outcomes, and that the learner need not always be in control. A key question for critics is, Are the demands that a constructivist learning environment places on the learner too great?

COMMUNICATIONS AND MEDIA THEORY

Communications theory is a field related to educational technology that has had an influence on pedagogical theory. Newby, Stepich, Lehman, and

Russell (1996) claim that communications theory dates back to Plato and Aristotle but became a recognized academic field only in the 1940s during World War II. Media theorists have analyzed the development of new media and how they are connected to broader social evolution. Mass communication theory was developed later in an attempt to understand how media function in influencing individuals, particularly in terms of political action. The first systematic study of communication in the United States occurred in the early 1930s in the form of public opinion surveys (Saettler, 1990). Although these theories are not the focus of this book, it is useful to examine them in regard to understanding computer learning environments as a new medium because they place the development in a larger historical context. Often in discussions about distance learning, it is easy to focus on the immediate issues connected with its development and lose sight of the long-term development of new media and technology.

RELATING THEORY TO SPECIFIC STUDY QUESTIONS

To better understand how sophisticated a particular institution is in its pedagogical approach to distance learning, a brief discussion of each of six key issues related to specific survey questions follows. (See Appendix A for survey questions.)

Interaction (Question 41)

The degree to which students interact with each other and with the instructor is one measure of academic quality. The amount of interactions, as well as its nature and quality, is important in evaluating the effectiveness of a distance learning program. We will see that in the qualitative results of this study, institutional representatives have given a lot of thought to this key question. A common complaint about correspondence courses in the past focused on the lack of direct or even indirect interaction with the faculty member. Furthermore, self-study format courses are often designed in such a way as to completely preclude interaction among students. Consequently, those who indicate a lower concern with interactivity likely have less evolved pedagogical approaches.

Collaboration (Question 42)

Research shows that a sense of community in distance learning courses can be created through team formation and group projects (Berg, 1999). While this may not be possible for every distance learning course on every subject, an understanding of this principle can go a long way toward creating a sense of community in these courses. Furthermore, by defining the nature of educational communities as being based on common purpose, and based on an examination of the research on virtual teams, it is clear that virtual learning teams should be structured around common projects and interdependent tasks. Institutions that are aware of the research on teams and who make conscious efforts to include group projects and team formation into the structure of their courses are likely to have more advanced pedagogical approaches.

Simulations/Case Studies (Question 43)

Simulations are a major part of the literature on human-computer interaction (HCI), particularly as it applies to educational environments (Pickover, 1991). Especially in educational environments, simulation can be a very effective tool. Because of the rich multimedia computer environment, learners can better bridge the gap between reality and the simulated task. Learning by doing is accomplished through simulation and is especially useful where actual environments are expensive and impractical to re-create constantly. Simulation is effective because it can create a context for learning (Feifer, 1994). Pickover (1991) encourages the use of the computer as an instrument for both simulation and discovery, particularly in science. Schank (1997) argues that using computer simulations, or virtual learning, offers the best opportunity for students to learn by doing in an apprenticeship-type model. He states that one of the biggest issues for learners is their fear of failing in public, while computers offer them an ability to fail independently. Schank focuses on the use of stories and/or case studies in simulations, and the use of both expert and nonexpert storytelling in simulations. Feifer (1994) argues that the difficulty of creating good simulations and the trouble learners sometimes have using simulations by themselves are two factors limiting the use of computer simulations in teaching. Consequently, we will find that few institutions in this study use simulation extensively.

Simulations and case studies represent two of the more advanced pedagogical approaches to distance learning. Institutions involved particularly in the wide use of simulations are likely to be among the most advanced. Case studies are related pedagogically to simulations because they use a narrative format to illustrate problems. We will find in the interviews that case studies are often used in distance learning business school programs since they are a usual part of that curriculum.

Navigation (Question 44)

One common problem faced by computer users generally is a tendency to get lost in the thread of hypertext links in a computer-based or online piece of software. Plowman (1996) claims that navigational practices in computer programs work against the coherence of the learning experience, causing it to be very fragmented and disorganized. For Plowman, user control of the narrative experience is reassuring, but confusing. The demands of interactivity requiring students to respond correctly in order to progress, the simultaneous use of multiple media, and the stress of interpreting icons and other interface conventions are all examples of practices in computer-based educational programs that interfere with learning. Plowman claims that one of the main problems is that interactivity at this point in the development of technology is "meager" in comparison to everyday human interaction. Real classroom interaction involves opportunities for customization and the addressing of specific learning problems on an ongoing basis. In addition, interactivity sometimes works against learners in that they are less likely to reflect on tasks before acting.

Hypertext is an important issue in HCI research. It is connected to the literature on cognitive issues because hypertext is said to mimic the associative manner in which the brain works. It is often argued that hypertext may alter the way people read, write, and organize information, and it may be crucial in the development of nonlinear thinking (McKnight, Dillon & Richardson, 1991). This research literature claims that linear text limits an author's ability to address the range of needs and interests of readers. Hypertext solves this problem, the argument goes, by presenting material in a nonlinear arrangement linked by key phrases in the text (Osgood, 1994). However, the research literature shows that one of the primary problems with hypertext is that it causes severe difficulty with navigation for users (McKnight, Dillon & Richardson, 1991; Osgood, 1994). If an institution is actively addressing this issue itself rather than leaving it up to a software vendor to solve the problem, it is an indication of pedagogical sophistication.

Tutoring (Question 45)

The tutoring function occurs in distance learning in two formats: human and machine. Human tutoring in distance learning is seen in institutions as diverse as the British Open University, Saybrook Institute, and Florida State University, all of which rely heavily on a formal tutor system to support their distance learning efforts. At its best, distance learning can take on the shape of one-on-one tutoring with rich and prompt feedback from faculty members guiding student work. Institutions that have designed courses emphasizing this format report consistent success.

Additionally, through computer-based materials, distance learning courses often take on a tutorial format. Probably one of the most exciting tools for learning is in the development of "intelligent tutors," or "computer agents." As many have noted, the application of Dewey's educational philosophy puts an enormous load on the teacher, one that is impractical for a broad-based application. Computers have the potential of meeting this need for labor through the development of intelligent tutors. Many of the programs thus far developed as tutors in training applications have been behaviorist in orientation. B. F. Skinner promoted the notion of teaching machine as tutor in pacing students through appropriate-level material, and through prompting, hinting, and suggesting ways students can arrive at correct answers. Partly, this behaviorist tendency has developed because of the limitations of the software itself. However, as research in intelligent tutors and artificial intelligence advances, this might change. Such change is already apparent in the area of intelligent agents for research. Applied to the Internet, intelligent agents can track the tendencies of the user and then collect information that fits the user's interests. While it may be true that artificial intelligence will never reach the point where it can serve as a tutor on the level of a human teacher, techniques such as the incorporation of randomness and intelligent agents customized to fit the user's interests may serve as useful tools approximating the function of a tutor.

The perceived value of the tutor relationship set up in distance learning courses and the potential for computers to augment this further are more indicators of pedagogical sophistication.

Media Richness (Question 46)

Although certainly print-based correspondence courses have been effective for over a hundred years in American higher education, the use of diverse media is a sign of sophistication in approach to distance learning. Institutions indicating that taking their distance learning courses most closely resembles reading are likely to be closer to the correspondence model. Conversely, those indicating that their courses more closely resemble film or television are using richer media and therefore are likely to have more complex approaches to course pedagogy. It will be seen later in the discussion of the survey and interviews that it is quite common for institutions to use multiple media in course delivery. While employing a combination of media may denote confusion or be a symptom of technological change, it also likely signals at the least an attempt to use more pedagogically complex materials.

CONCLUSION

The research literature shows that one could take either side of the behaviorism versus constructivism debate in relationship to technology and present a convincing argument. Clearly, each approach has advantages for certain subjects and certain types of learners. However, the technology cannot be separated from the theory. According to some of the research literature, one of the problems with technology-enabled learning is that it has been used to automate unsuccessful teaching strategies. Clearly, the use of technology in education will be successful only to the degree it applies effective learning theories.

Not surprisingly, distance learning theory is very much a reflection of general learning theory as it has developed over time. In fact, it is remarkable how little has been written on the unique learning theories as they may apply to various forms of distance learning. Clearly, much needs to be done to further the research agenda on the pedagogy of distance learning. We will see that while some interview respondents are very thoughtful about using new approaches to teaching with distance learning, often these important questions are left to licensed software companies and individual faculty with little special training. To properly evaluate the sophistication of an institution's approach to distance learning pedagogy, a general understanding of research in this field is needed. Indicators of how institutional motivation to adopt distance learning affects pedagogical approaches are seen in such factors as course development, use of specific technologies, and advanced teaching approaches and strategies. The next chapter addresses the literature on market approaches to higher education in an effort to understand how these may connect to both motivation for use and administrative practice.

CHAPTER 4

Review of Literature on Market Approaches to Administration in Higher Education

To what degree is the influence of corporate approaches to administration shaping the way distance learning in higher education is implemented and managed?

This chapter focuses on market approaches to university administration to help clarify the way this trend might play a part in the motivation to use distance learning. Evidence of market model approaches to distance learning should be apparent in data showing attempts to reduce labor expenses through technology, copyright practices giving universities an accumulation of fixed intellectual capital, administrative approaches involving collaborations with businesses, and corporate decision-making styles. When looking at current trends toward market models in higher education, it is useful to analyze the historical context for proprietary and vocational school education, similarities and differences between these schools and traditional higher education, demographic and other characteristics of the schools and their students, curriculum, and staffing. Finally, this topic has become the center of a heated debate about the mechanization and commercialization of the academy, and consequently a rich literature on the subject has developed.

HISTORY OF APPLIED, VOCATIONAL,
AND PROPRIETARY HIGHER EDUCATION

From its origin, higher education has had an interest in the practical application of knowledge—the earliest universities were dedicated to training students for law, civil, and religious careers. According to Noble (1997), the first academy to formally pursue useful aims was the Italian Accademia dei Lincei, formed in 1603 with the stated purpose of improving the knowledge of natural science. In 1660 the Royal Society of London was founded with similar expectations. Wilms (1974) claims that vocational education began in America in Plymouth Colony as early as 1635. Over the years, the belief in technology and in practical arts has pushed higher education in America in the direction of vocational education. A prime example of this emphasis is the landmark Morrill Act of 1862, setting forth the system for public higher education in America. The Morrill Act offered each state 30,000 acres of public land for every member of Congress from that state, with the land to be sold and proceeds invested as a permanent endowment for at least one college designated by the state legislature. The colleges founded or designated under this act were required to stress agriculture, the mechanic arts, and the military arts. The overall objective was to educate "industrial classes" in professions (Rudolph, 1962).

Proprietary education is often linked in the literature to vocational education because most of these for-profit schools have a practical curriculum. Academic researchers in education have largely ignored proprietary education. The research literature shows that higher education in general looks at proprietary schools with suspicion, mistrust, and outright disdain. Most authors in the literature look to correspondence instruction as the first type of vocational training to be conducted privately. As early as 1728, home study courses in shorthand were offered. Private resident schools became common sometime in the early eighteenth century where classes took place at a business or home, usually on practical programs such as business, surveying, mathematics, and navigation. However, the real growth of vocational education began in the early nineteenth century with the increased need for skilled trades. Mechanic institutes began to spring up when the Lyceum Movement, patterned after the French system and dedicated to practical instruction, arrived in America. The earliest of these schools was the Gardner Lyceum in Maine which opened in 1823 offering courses in farming, navigation, and carpentry. The rise of vocational schools is said to have occurred through the rapid industrialization of the United States combined with the inefficiency of the limited apprentice system. Many large proprietary schools grew in the nineteenth century, the largest being the Bryant-Stratton chain, founded in 1852 (Lee & Merisotis, 1990).

Henry (1943) defines vocational education as "learning how to work." According to Thompson (1973), the history of vocational education has been an effort to improve technical competence and to raise an individual's position in society through mastering his environment with technology. Additionally, vocational education is geared to the needs of the job market and thus is often seen as contributing to national economic strength. Historically, vocational education and apprenticeships were done simply through a father passing on his knowledge of particular skills to his son. This tradition might be viewed as the informal beginning of vocational education. In eighteenth-century America, skilled labor was concentrated on the East Coast. As a result, a technology gap existed in the Midwest and the western United States. Vocational education programs developed to close this gap. In terms of demographics, initially most of the students in vocational programs had not graduated from high school, but by the 1930s, 64% were graduates. Additionally, at first the majority of the students were men, until women entered the schools seeking cosmetology training. Although the influx of veterans into the university after World War II had a significant impact, less than one-third of GI Bill students went to a college or university. Instead, they attended on-the-job training, farm training, or proprietary schools (Lee & Merisotis, 1990).

The military and war efforts contributed greatly to the further development of American vocational education. During World War I, the Federal Board for Vocational Education worked with the army to determine the need for an estimated 200,000 mechanics, then found them suitable training. In World War II, existing vocational education systems greatly helped in providing trained inductees for the war effort. On the public policy level, the Smith-Hughes Act of 1917 defined and provided support for vocational education (Henry, 1943). Compulsory public education began with the Supreme Court ruling in *Meyer v. Nebraska* (1923), which ruled that the state could compel children to attend school and could establish standards. This decision effectively brought vocational education into the mandatory public school system. The Vocational Education Act of 1963 was significant because it expanded and redirected the federal investment in vocational education (Thompson, 1973).

While liberal arts education focuses on the development of the whole person, vocational education centers on one particular work skill. Unlike traditional higher education, vocational education tends to change rapidly because it depends on technology and meeting labor needs. Consequently, Thompson (1973) sees the most significant development in the history of vocational education as the change in occupational structure from an emphasis on heavy industries to service occupations. As a result of this transformation, the separation between the traditional liberal arts curriculum and vocational education has narrowed.

However, the differences between the management of proprietary schools and traditional higher education institutions are great. In proprietary schools, the owners or corporate directors are more likely to make critical decisions regarding the direction of the school, program mix, admissions, or other academic standards. Conversely, nonprofit and government institutions respond to stakeholders and consequently have more layers of decision-making. Faculty influence in proprietary schools is minimal, facilities are often leased, extracurricular activities are not emphasized, and there is no residential element (Lee & Merisotis, 1990). Scheduling at proprietary schools varies from 8 to 152 weeks, whereas universities typically have quarters and semesters. Nevertheless, this distinction is changing as universities with programs focused on adult learners move to shorter terms. In general, studies show that students of proprietary schools are more likely to be low income, female, and members of a minority group than traditional university students. Finally, proprietary schools are generally regulated by state licensing, rather than regional accreditation agencies (Lee & Merisotis, 1990).

Wilms (1974) argues that vocational education has a single purpose, preparing students for successful employment, and that placement is a key aspect of vocational education. He describes the characteristics of vocational education as cost-effective management, often breaking courses into short units or topics, and with a concentration on teaching without tenure. Vocational education is rooted in the marketplace, while public institutions tend to change more slowly to protect the internal order of the institution. Wilms claims that public universities in particular are less flexible in meeting student and employer needs because they also fulfill institutional and governmental needs.

Financial aid for vocational education was a key reason for the increased development of proprietary training in the twentieth century. Starting with the Veterans Education Benefits program after World War II, and continuing with student aid, proprietary school students have used government grants and loans to encourage enrollment in their programs. The watershed 1972 Amendments to the Higher Education Act provided full and equal participation with traditional higher education students. This single change in public policy was very controversial and led to charges against for-profit vocational education institutions of recruitment and false marketing abuses and lack of quality control by higher education institutions.

In the mid-1980s, proprietary school students were identified as having higher default rates on student loans than borrowers from other sectors. As one-fourth of all federal student aid went to these students, government officials became concerned with this problem. In their defense, proprietary schools explained the data by pointing out that their students were higher risks for loan default to begin with (Lee & Merisotis, 1990).

In evaluating the effectiveness of vocational education, evidence (Wilms, 1974) indicates that proprietary schools recruit and hold students with fewer resources than do public schools. Public and proprietary school students have similar success in the job market. However, students have a more negative impression of vocational education, as greater numbers of proprietary school students claim that they would not repeat training. According to Wilms (1974), vocational school students may be more critical of their proprietary schools because of the higher cost for training. More troubling is Wilms' claim that eight out of ten graduates of vocational education programs in technical-level jobs did not get the jobs for which they were trained. Additionally, eight out of ten graduates from lower-level programs did get the jobs they trained for but barely earned the minimum wage.

The literature on vocational education is important to this study because many of the attitudes toward distance learning are rooted in the historical connection between correspondence instruction and vocational education. Many of the attitudes toward proprietary and vocational schools may be extended to distance learning because of its often applied curriculum and connection to for-profit institutions. Additionally, the association of distance learning with university extension divisions, and with more applied curricula aimed at adult learners, further cements this connection with vocational education.

SOCIAL AND PHILOSOPHICAL
LITERATURE ON TECHNOLOGY

A long and complex literature on the philosophical and social aspects of the use of technology in society is relevant to this discussion because it gives us a deeper sense of the context in which distance learning is regarded in academic settings. Cooper (1995) suggests that a positive viewpoint in the literature on technology and philosophy is that technological advancements can lead to political freedom and alleviate mass poverty, while a negative viewpoint suggests that technology narrows self-understanding. According to Mitcham and Mackey (1972), technology is often connected to practical skills, or what has been described here as vocational education.

A more critical tradition includes Romantics such as Jean-Jacques Rousseau arguing that technology is an outgrowth of a lust for power. This notion of technology as the pursuit of power leads to its being perceived as inherently evil in some of the literature on technology. A central question in this literature is whether technology is a means to liberation or an extension of man's desire for power and dominance.

A tradition of historical criticism with roots in a Marxist class analysis views technology as a tool of dominance by the advantaged class. This viewpoint applied to distance learning leads to an understanding of technology use in higher education as a means toward the end of dominance by administrators and trustees. In *Technics and Civilization*, Mumford (1934) argues that men became mechanical before they built complicated machines. He sees the history of the machine as one of both liberation and oppression, with Romanticism an attempt to move the machine out of the center of human society. Mumford views the problem with Romanticism in its failure to distinguish between good and bad uses of machines. He sees the motivation for the use of machines as a deliberate effort to achieve a mechanical way of life and power. Mumford claims that the main human motive is to serve the machine, as a kind of religion or a compulsive urge toward mechanical life. Mumford sees the clock as the most important machine because it synchronized the actions of men and replaced the notion of religious eternity with mechanical time. Capitalism used the machine not to further social good, but as a tool to increase private profit, with consumption leading to what he describes as "purposeless materialism." In examining the history of the machine, he argues that war was the chief propagator of the machine. The mechanical model derived from war led to the army as the ideal form of industry (Mumford, 1934). This explains the widespread use of military terminology in business.

TECHNOLOGY AND MEDIA THEORY

Connected firmly with the more general philosophical literature analyzing the role of technology in society is a body of literature on technology and media theory. In terms of communication media, Mumford (1934) saw the printed sheet as the first completely mechanical achievement. Writing was a great labor-saving device compared to oral communication and released people from a dependence on the present time. Harold Innis (1972; 1991), another leading figure in the analysis of the political and historical impact of communication forms on civilization, argues that studying forms of communication brings forth an understanding of government and the rise and fall of empires. He sees changes in political form coinciding with adoption of new media. Thus the shift in Egyptian civilization from monarchy to a more democratic organization coincided with a shift in emphasis from stone to papyrus. The properties of the dominant medium, along with institutional structure, facilitate knowledge and power.

Innis proposes that time and space are two key characteristics of communication: media that emphasize time are durable in character, while media that emphasize space are less durable and lighter in character. He claims materials that emphasize time, such as parchment, clay, and stone, favor decentralization because of the difficulty of reproducing and distributing them; those that emphasize space, such as papyrus and paper, favor centralization because they are more easily duplicated and used to spread communications. Media based on space are suited to enterprises involving administration and trade covering wide geographic areas. Thus, Rome's use of papyrus became the basis of a large administrative empire. Empires flourish under conditions in which civilization reflects the influence of more than one medium, where the bias of one medium toward centralization is offset by the bias of another medium toward centralization. Innis argues that monopolies of knowledge develop and decline partly in relation to the medium of communication on which they were built, and tend to rise or fall as they emphasize decentralization or centralization and time or space. Use of the parchment codex gave Christians an enormous advantage over other religions. Since material for early cultures needed to be recopied, an extensive censorship developed. The monopoly over the Bible and the Latin language was destroyed by the printing press. According to Innis, the subsequent increasing influence of print has been reflected in a bias toward government documents and the rights of the individual.

Innis promotes the use of dialogue as a form of communication. He argues that the dialogues of Plato were developed as an effective instrument for preserving the power of the spoken word. The oral tradition is important because it emphasizes dialogue and works against monopolies of knowledge. Furthermore, the oral tradition emphasizes the spirit, while writing and printing are inherently materialistic (this is ironic given his claim about the importance of the parchment codex in the spread of Christianity). Aware of John Dewey and Robert Park's work in the Chicago School, Innis argued for a revival of the oral tradition in education.

DEBATE ON THE COMMERCIALIZATION OF HIGHER EDUCATION

Although it may seem to be a recent trend, fear of commercialization in higher education did not begin in the 1980s. In fact, one might argue that fear of commercialization in American higher education has its roots in early efforts to make the curriculum more practical and in the so-called Yale Report of 1828, which was a reaction to the trend toward a more applied curriculum, promoting instead a return to a course of study based on the classics. In modern times, Veblen argued in *The Higher Learning in America* (1954) that the university president is the main channel whereby business values enter the university. His book is a critique of pragmatism and vocationalism, and a criticism of the president's role in leading America down this path. Veblen sees the principles of business organization—the focus on control and achievement—applied increasingly to learning. The motivation: universities seek utilitarian management to pursue endowments, and this approach works because practical knowledge is valued most in society. In contrast to this trend, Veblen argued that the two primary purposes of the university are scholarly inquiry and the instruction of students. In more recent times, the debate can be traced to Robert Nisbet's 1971 book *The Degradation of the Academic Dogma*, a criticism of how government-sponsored research was affecting the university.

Although one can see that the debate over the applied nature of the curriculum, the use of technology, and the connection to business is not new, it became increasingly heated in the latter half of the twentieth century. However, while much has been written recently about university-business partnerships, Bowie (1994) points out that the two cultures developed together in America. Changes in university patent policies in the 1970s helped pave the way for cooperative relationships, and universities had a clear economic incentive to establish partnerships with businesses. Bowie claims that in the 1990s universities faced both financial trouble and increased public scrutiny. Additionally, there was the perception that the United States had lost technological advantage on a global scale. Partnerships with businesses were seen as an opportunity to meet these challenges.

In the 1980s, the National Center for Science created prominent programs such as the Industry-University Cooperative Research Projects Program and the Industry-University Cooperative Research Centers Program. The Research Roundtable was founded in 1984 to provide a forum where representatives from industry, education, and government could explore ways to improve research productivity. Gene splicing was achieved by academics, and the key patents for the products of DNA technologies were owned by universities. Commercial applications were obvious from the start. Additionally, universities began venture-capital activities, investing in the inventions of faculty. Also, corporations began paying universities such as MIT for their expertise through an annual retainer fee for consulting services (Bowie, 1994).

In *The Monster Under the Bed*, Davis and Botkin (1995) argue that we are seeing a transition of higher education from government control to business control as the needs of students change and the role of education moves increasingly toward job preparation. On local, state, national, and international scales, the demand for higher education is pushing universities to become more productive and efficient. Consequently, public policy makers are looking increasingly toward business for answers.

While much of the focus of concern has been on the commercialization of research activities within the university, increasingly the basic teaching/learning function is also being transformed by commercial forces. John Sperling, the founder of the University of Phoenix, sees a nontraditional graduate student population of 880,000 as a primary reason for the development of proprietary educational models. This group is described as over 25 years old, working full time, and seeking a professional master's or doctoral degree. Furthermore, these students comprise an especially good market because 42% of employers who offer it as a fringe benefit put no dollar limit on tuition reimbursement (Sperling & Tucker, 1997). Sperling and Tucker argue that because taxpayers heavily subsidize not only public but also independent higher education institutions, both types of institutions are often subject to criticisms of poor productivity and inefficiency. They cite a *New York Times* article, "One Top College's Price Tag: Why So Low and So High?" (July 27, 1994), in estimating a $19,285 per student per year taxpayer subsidy to support Swarthmore undergraduate education. Sperling and Tucker argue that for-profit, adult-centered institutions' advantages are that they use less federal and state tax money, provide access to private capital for start-up funds and expansion, operate from leased commercial office space, quickly respond to the market, have a more focused product, relate well to for-profit businesses, are close to the customer, and have a service orientation. Furthermore, they are well managed; the faculty are working professionals and consequently are constructive agents of change; they offer a year-round schedule and faster graduation for students.

Sperling and Tucker (1997) hold that the corporate structure allows the University of Phoenix model to maintain and enhance the curriculum. Additionally, the market model encourages innovation and the discipline that for-profit aims demand. If for-profit institutions are so clearly more efficient than traditional higher education, why aren't there more? Sperling sees public policy and accrediting institutions as constructed barriers to entry, keeping for-profit universities from entering all states.

Burton Clark (1998) perceives more and different types of students looking for a growing array of subjects at universities. Government expects universities to do much more for society and at the same time is becoming an "unreliable patron." Clark sees a deepening asymmetry between environmental demand and institutional capability. In his 1998 book, which profiles a group of entrepreneurial European universities, Clark identifies five elements innovative universities use to transform themselves into entrepreneurial institutions: a strengthened leadership core, an expanded developmental periphery, a diversified funding base, a stimulated academic base, and an integrated entrepreneurial culture.

Clark's point of view on university-business partnerships is decidedly more positive than that of academic critics such as Slaughter, Leslie, and Bowie. He sees at successful institutions a blending of management and academic values, with strong faculty involvement. Central faculty involvement is a crucial step in avoiding the appearance of top-down management approaches. In response to criticisms that business-university partnerships lead to a lack of attention to basic research, Clark claims that when carried out effectively, a widespread embodiment of entrepreneurship in a university strengthens growth in other units. Successful university-business partnerships occur when organizations diversify income to increase financial resources, provide discretionary money, and reduce governmental dependency. On the administrative end, these partnerships, if done correctly, develop new units outside traditional departments, evolve beliefs that guide rational structural changes, and build a central leadership capacity. Finally, in opposition to the fear of a leveling of universities through these partnerships, Clark argues that entrepreneurial responses in universities lead to greater individualization and differentiation of one institution from another (Clark, 1998).

In turning to distance learning and specifically this larger criticism of both the de-humanizing influence of technology and the commercialization of higher education, David Noble is a primary voice. Noble (1998) argues that the trend is a battle between students and professors on one side, and university administrations and companies with "educational products" on the other. He sees distance learning as a trend toward the old era of mass production:

> What is driving this headlong rush to implement new technology with so little regard for deliberation of the pedagogical and economic costs and at the risk of student and faculty alienation and opposition? A short answer might be the fear of getting left behind, the incessant pressures of "progress." But there is more to it. For the universities are not simply undergoing a technological transformation. Beneath that change, and camouflaged by it, lies another: the commercialization of higher education. (Noble, 1998, p. 1)

Noble sees a trend over the last twenty years toward the commodification of, first, research, and now, through distance learning, teaching/learning. He claims that university administrators are motivated to use distance learning in order to gain revenue for their institutions and themselves.

In a broader sense, Noble (1997) views the present enchantment with things technological as being rooted in religious myths. Noble's more general interest in the history of technology and what he describes as the "religion of technology" focuses on how modern technology and faith are merged. In the social-philosophical tradition of Mumford and Innis, he believes that the technological enterprise is an essentially religious endeavor. Noble argues that mankind needs to learn to reject other-worldly dreams of technological promise in order to redirect human effort toward more human ends.

Since distance learning can involve partnerships with for-profit organizations, can be viewed as a route to increased revenue, and potentially can be used to reduce labor expenses, it is naturally tied to what Slaughter and Leslie (1997) term "academic capitalism." Slaughter and Leslie identify the changing economics of higher education defined by a decrease in unrestricted funding and subsequent increased dependence on external funding sources for universities. Although Slaughter and Leslie's critique focuses primarily on the applied sciences, the overall trend certainly isn't limited to those disciplines. Case studies in their work show that academic capitalism is not confined to science and engineering, but cuts across other units (Slaughter & Leslie, 1997).

Overall, Slaughter (1990) sees the higher education policy literature as undertheorized. A more class-conscious analysis of the development of market models of higher education would perceive unentitled groups pressing for the expansion of higher education as a way of improving their class position. In response, representatives of elite institutions attempt to constrict easy access to maintain control and to perpetuate class privilege. As businesses become more competitive and have slimmer profit margins, national and state capital is spent to meet business rather than social needs. Additionally, as education costs soared in the 1980s, many business groups, aided by major foundations, were mobilized. Because of the corporate community's greater organization and effort, as well as the U.S. position in the global market, the voice of the corporate community is heard more in the higher education policy-making process.

Slaughter (1990) examined a corporate advocacy group called the Business-Higher Education Forum in profiling the activities of businesses in changing public higher education. She claims that the organizational rhetoric of economic priorities and plans for allocation of resources contradict the group's stated concern with expanding access and equal educational opportunity. Slaughter points out that because more monies will be concentrated on fewer elite research institutions, less may be available for expanding access and career opportunities. She claims that the Forum agenda is tax policy, antitrust legislation, intellectual property laws, and the use of government to organize business interests and provide resources.

Slaughter warns that privatization of higher education transfers what was once part of the public domain to the private. She sees corporate-university partnerships as inherently antidemocratic. Slaughter argues that there is very little empirical evidence of direct linkages between university research and industrial innovation. Furthermore, corporate investment in universities is not as great as is generally thought. Although the relationship is presented as mutually beneficial, corporations actually dominate because the university is asked to direct its resources to meet corporate ends.

One of the early concerns in these partnerships was that academic publication would be delayed or prevented because of copyright protection. Additionally, such relationships move the university's attention from basic science to product development. Faculty organizations began to express concern with university-business collaborations, as highlighted in a 1983 American Association of University Professors (AAUP) report, "Corporate Funding of Academic Research." Conflict of interest fears also arise when faculty members with financial interests in companies may be influenced to misrepresent or conceal discoveries. However, according to Slaughter and Leslie (1997), conflict of interest discussions are hampered by a lack of clear definition.

For Slaughter (1990), universities are willing to enter into partnerships with industry because of the promise of profit. University leaders see university-industry research partnerships as an alternative source of unrestricted funds for their institutions, particularly when they can make claims on the intellectual property produced. Slaughter references Derek Bok in speaking about university-industry partnerships negotiated around the commercial exploitation of basic research as the "new" service. The modern research university is resource dependent and looks to business and government for funding. Increased corporate support lessens university dependence on the political process and government funding.

Bok (1991) expresses concern that if the university is perceived as a commercial enterprise, then its stakeholders may change the nature of their relationship to the university for the worse. He is troubled that in the public's eyes, the traditional university desire to seek the truth and disseminate knowledge might be supplanted by the profit motive. Bok argues that as universities grow more aggressive in seeking funding, their image changes, thus making it harder to appear to be nonprofit institutions. Additionally, there is a danger that academic departments will be viewed as profit centers in a business model. As a result, there is the fear that research centers undercut university governance by moving power away from departments.

On the other hand, Bowie (1994) claims that the biggest problem may be that such partnerships may not work. University-business partnerships cannot be counted on to provide funding for universities. In fact, they may end up costing universities money. According to Bowie, only 1 in 10 patented discoveries recovers the money spent on filing the patent, only 1 in 100 makes between $20,000 and $50,000, and only 1 in 1,000 is a major money-maker. In evaluating whether universities should enter into partnership agreements with businesses, Bowie argues that the practical question becomes which model is more productive, research directed by the discipline of the market, or research based on the efforts of a group of individual faculty members?

ECONOMICS OF DISTANCE LEARNING

It is useful to look at economic models of distance learning to better understand the forces shaping the debate on the commercialization of higher education. Bates (1995) argues that each type of distance learning has a different economic model. Broadcast and computer-based learning formats are more expensive per student, while print-based and online forms are less expensive up front. However, beyond 1,000 students, the expense variance among the types of distance learning formats narrows considerably. Although there are differences in the economics among the types of technologies used in distance learning, they all involve to varying degrees the following two basic approaches to faculty: replacement of labor with capital, and replacement of faculty with cheaper labor.

John Daniel, vice-chancellor of the British Open University, claims that the basic economic approach of distance learning is to replace labor with capital, or to replace variable costs with fixed costs. He proposes that the per unit cost of teaching can be cut either by adding more students to existing courses or by making instruction more efficient (Daniel, 1998). Daniel shows that there is a point at which volume is large enough for distance learning courses to be more productive than traditional courses by replacing labor with fixed-cost capital. The British Open University claims that it has used this model to reduce faculty labor costs from 66% to 20% of the total budget (Bates, 1995).

In the United States, economic models for distance learning in higher education at the degree level are still being developed (Massy & Zemsky, 1995; Twigg, 1996). *Dollars, Distance, and Online Education: The New Economics of College Teaching and Learning* (2000), edited by Finkelstein, Frances, Jewett, and Scholz, offers the most complete description to date. In this collection, Jewett (2000) follows Daniel in arguing that distance learning offers economies of scale after an up-front capital investment. He claims that savings can only be realized by reducing personnel costs. Jewett sees the solution in finding ways to "unbundle" faculty tasks and reduce labor costs. There is some evidence that this process may be occurring. The Primary Research Group (1999) found in its survey that instructor/tutor salaries account for only 31.72% of the distance learning program expenses. However, Finkelstein and Scholz (2000) maintain that research shows that mega-universities with large enrollments are cost-effective, but that small distance learning programs do not show such cost savings. Maitland, Hendrickson, and Dubeck (2000) contend that only large courses with more sections than one faculty member can teach at a time offer savings. Pumerantz and Frances (2000) argue that conventional economic models do not take into account how the lack of face-to-face interaction in distance learning instruction affects learning and student satisfaction. Caplan (2000) concurs with this assessment and points out that research typically focuses on students with no other possible access to higher education, and that when distance learning is optional it is viewed as inferior to face-to-face instruction. If this reduced student satisfaction is taken into account, the perceived economic benefit may be more difficult to justify.

Are distance learning programs reducing the amount of faculty labor in American higher education? Some (Massy & Zemsky, 1995; Daniel, 1998) point out that in practice, technology is often added to a fixed faculty cost, thereby only adding expense to the total budget. Metlitzky (1999) surveyed faculty and found that they disagreed with the notion that technology reduces the faculty workload, confirming the impression that labor is not currently being reduced by the forms of distance learning being utilized in the United States. Consequently, from the research literature it is unclear whether or not the model of replacing labor with capital is leading to a reduction in faculty workload in American higher education at this time.

The second basic approach, a labor-for-labor model, is to divide the faculty role into segments and reduce the total labor cost by replacing higher-priced faculty with less expensive labor. Jewett (1999) identifies three basic functions of faculty in a cost analysis: preparation, presentation, and interaction/assessment. To the degree that these functions can be performed individually by less expensive labor, the overall cost will be reduced. The British Open University divides up these functions with course design teams and 7,000 part-time tutors (associate lecturers) whose tasks are to provide academic support to local groups of students (Daniel, 1998). Daniel cites Snowden and Daniel (1980) for an equation that expresses this division of faculty roles:

$$C = a1 \times 1 + a2 \times 2 + by + c$$

Where:

C = total cost;

a1 = course development cost per credit;

×1 = course credits in development;

a2 = course revision/maintenance/replacement costs per credit;

×2 = course credits in delivery;

b = delivery costs per course enrollment;

y = course enrollments;

c = institutional overheads. (Daniel, 1998, p. 63)

What is telling in this formula is that there is no separate symbol for faculty compensation. Faculty expenses are spread among development, maintenance, and delivery costs, and in this way the formula represents the way the faculty expense is dispersed in the economic model. In America, Arvan et al. (1998) argue for a labor-for-labor model, similar to the British model.

These distance learning economic models show that faculty rates of compensation and duties may be affected either by substituting labor with capital or by using less expensive labor to perform current faculty tasks. With this understanding of the economics of distance learning, the more refined questions then are, To what degree at present in American higher education is (1) faculty labor being replaced by capital, and (2) faculty labor being replaced by less expensive labor performing roles traditionally performed by faculty?

CONCLUSION

The question this book addresses is, To what degree are economic models and corporate influences behind the use of distance learning in higher education? Indicators in the survey shining light on institutional approaches to this question include faculty compensation, copyright practices, collaborations with for-profit entities, budgets, and revenue expectations for distance learning. While much of the argument about the commercialization of higher education focuses on the sciences and traditional university operations, this concern is also very much evident in reactions to the implementation of distance learning in higher education.

This research literature review of market approaches to university administration shows that a long and heated debate has been waged over how applied the curriculum should be, the appropriate relationship of business to the university, and the general influence of the use of technology on society—particularly a key social organization such as the university. Thus it is important to consider the way in which this debate might play a part in the motivation to use, or not use, distance learning.

CHAPTER 5

Research Methodology

Some academics who write about research methods suggest that studies may benefit from a combined quantitative and qualitative approach (Campbell & Stanley, 1966; Gorden, 1975). The benefits are that data sets can be compared for consistency, and the interviews can allow some insight into the causal processes, while the surveys can provide indication of the prevalence of the phenomenon. Consequently, the methodology for this study consists of two parts: a questionnaire emphasizing quantitative responses sent to administrators of distance learning programs, and the qualitative portion, consisting of interviews of representatives at a sample of institutions.

For the purposes of this study, distance learning format courses are defined as having at least a 50% reduction in contact time (as traditionally required at the particular institution) through use of any technology or medium. Three primary lists of distance learning providers were used for the quantitative part of the study: *Peterson's Guide to Distance Learning Courses* (UCEA, 2000), *Peterson's Independent Study Catalog* (UCEA, 1999), and *Campus-Free College Degrees: Thorson's Guide to Accredited Distance Learning Degree Programs* (Thorson, 1999). The lists were combined and duplicates eliminated.

In the first mailing, 1,114 emailed surveys were sent out. However, only 623 (55.9%) of the emailed survey were sent directly to individuals; the rest went to generic department or university information addresses. Of those emailed surveys, 295 were returned nondeliverable. Five institutions responded that they did not have distance learning courses as defined in the study; four others declined to participate for various reasons. The final number of completed surveys returned was 176. If the returned emails are excluded, this constitutes a response rate of 21.5%. As the original list was quite comprehensive, including virtually all the higher education institutions in the United States using distance learning to any significant degree, this response is quite good. Additionally, in comparison to other national surveys of distance learning, which are based on smaller samples (such as the ITC, NEA, and Primary Research Group surveys), this response should be deemed sufficient.

In addition to this quantitative sample, the qualitative portion of the study was expanded. Instead of the 4 institutions originally planned to be studied through interviews, 17 were done. The reasons for this expansion were that the data gathered from the initial interviews were particularly rich and useful, and that institutions in fact were granting their cooperation. A question was added to the computerized survey for respondents to indicate if they would be available for follow-up interviews. This strategy worked well, as many respondents agreed to phone interviews. Institutions were chosen for interviews based on two seemingly contradictory factors: first, the desire to get a cross section of types of institutions (spanning two-year, four-year, rural, urban, Research One, comprehensive, historically black colleges and universities [HBCU], religious, distance learning only, proprietary), and second, the institutions' uniqueness in terms of being leaders in the field. Additionally, the choice of institutions to study through interviews followed the return of the survey in order to try to help identify representative institutions and further probe issues identified through the quantitative data. As a result of this process, more doctoral degree–granting institutions were followed up with interviews than planned because of the large number of intriguing responses from these institutions. Additionally, since it was clear that specialized institutions were responding in great numbers, representatives from such institutions were chosen to interview.

The survey for the quantitative part of the research was completed through the Internet. The benefits of this approach were that the Internet is widely used in higher education, is more convenient than regular mail, and allows for much faster response time. Heflich and Rice (1999) found in their study that the Internet can even produce positive results in qualitative surveys through the encouragement of reflective dialogue. The process was to send an introductory email with a basic description of the project, presumably allaying concerns about such matters as sponsorship and confidentiality. The email was linked to a URL (uniform resource locator) where a computer form was used to collect the data on a remote server. The surveys were coded so that responses were tracked (except for a few who thwarted the coding system). A follow-up email was sent two weeks later to remind those who had not responded to complete the survey.

For the interviews, potential subjects were contacted by email. The questions focused on more in-depth probing of the primary and secondary questions of the study. The interviewees were asked to reserve 60 minutes for a single interview. Bernard (1988) suggests that in situations where the researcher has only one chance to interview, semi-structured interviewing is best. Accordingly, while there was a set of standard questions for each subject, it was intended that by design there would be flexibility to pursue other questions as indicated by the on-the-spot responses.

Because the literature on research methods suggests testing survey instruments before using them to determine usefulness and reliability (Marshall & Rossman, 1989), both the survey instrument and the interview protocol were tested on a small sample first. As a result, minor adjustments were made to both the survey and the interview questions.

According to Yin (1984), interviews should be used when "how" or "why" questions are posed, and when the focus is on a contemporary phenomenon within some real-life context. They were used in this study to provide a more textured understanding of distance learning practice than the questionnaire data could have returned. Most important, the interviews help with an understanding of why distance learning administration follows, or doesn't follow, particular patterns. Interview methods are useful in determining patterns and linkages and consequently are appropriate in understanding how distance learning is implemented in higher education. Furthermore, the interviews can serve to check the validity of the quantitative data.

Marshall and Rossman (1989) identify six basic decision areas in qualitative data collection: assumptions of qualitative approaches, sample selection logic, justification for design, data collection flexibility, acknowledgment of the intensive aspects of fieldwork, and consideration of ethical issues. Assumptions of the qualitative approach to this study include the notion that distance learning is implemented for a variety of reasons, that administrators and faculty responsible for distance learning are key interviewees, and that an interview approach can help with an understanding of why these types of programs are implemented as they are in a university setting. The logic of the sample selection is a desire to use a representative selection and one that is obtainable by the researcher. The justification for the design of the study is that quantitative and qualitative methods are needed to get at both the descriptive and the underlying data. Flexibility was built into the design of the interviews through an iterative process of continual refinement of the interviewing techniques based on experience. Because the interviewing was labor-intensive, the sampling, although larger than originally expected, was limited to 17 institutions. Finally, anonymity can be a key aspect of qualitative research if the information gathered is sensitive or current in nature. Rubin and Rubin (1995) suggest the use of informed consent statements describing the purposes of the research, background on the research, and disclosure of the benefits and risks for those involved. Such a form was used for the interviews, with participants required to sign the form to acknowledge an understanding of the risks (Appendices E & F). Furthermore, after the interviews, a post-interview form was used to grant permission for the use of attributed or unattributed quotes (as so noted on the form) (Appendix G).

ANALYSIS

The quantitative data were tabulated and analyzed to describe current practices and policy in higher education. Additionally, the data were analyzed through the perspective of the literature reviews on the pedagogy and management of distance learning. The population of higher education institutions offering distance learning credit courses is to a large extent known. However, because survey responses were depended upon for the data, inferential statistical methods were used to generalize about the whole population from the sample of respondents (Bernard, 1988; Healey, 1999). Consequently, measures of association in percentages and ratios to identify significant relationships between variables are used. In particular, I looked for relationships between indicators of market-model administration (such as self-described institutional motive, where courses are administratively housed, faculty compensation, partnerships with for-profit entities, consistency with organizational mission, marketing practices, overall economics, etc.). Additionally, the course development process (resources directed toward process, depth and sophistication of pedagogical issues addressed, use of licensed materials, faculty training, support student services, technical support, assessment, faculty oversight, etc.) is examined. Furthermore, relationships between individual variables and type of institution (two-year, four-year, public, independent) are of special interest. Also, connections between organizational structure variables, program size, and implementation history are of primary interest. Recognizing that any particular informant may slant data based on faculty/administration status, this variable is analyzed in connection with the other variables to look for significant differences in responses. SPSS software was used to tabulate and analyze the data to identify significant descriptive patterns and relationships among the variables.

Once the qualitative data were collected, the analytic process involved five basic modes, per Marshall and Rossman (1989): data organization, categorization, uncovering themes and patterns, testing and searching for alternative explanations of the data, and finally, writing the report. The qualitative data were coded using QSR N4 NUDIST software. Coding is the process of grouping interviewee responses into categories that bring together the similar ideas, concepts, or themes discovered (Rubin & Rubin, 1995; Bernard, 1988).

LIMITATIONS OF THE DATA

In regard to the study's limitations, it is important to note that those both surveyed and interviewed were primarily administrators. For the survey, 78.2% of respondents reported that they are classified as full-time administrators. While the interviews revealed that many full-time administrators had been faculty members at one time—this likely was also true of many completing the survey—the respondent's administrative background needs to be recognized in evaluating the results. In particular, views on broad issues such as institutional purpose and future applications of technology in higher education might very well be somewhat slanted. The data collected on more objective institutional practices are less likely to be affected by the position of respondents within the university. Nevertheless, this study is sufficiently broad in scope (as one can see from the list of 176 participating institutions) and depth (interviews with representatives from 17 institutions of various types) that the data clearly have some value for purposes of being able to extrapolate to a larger population of higher education institutions.

CHAPTER

Institutional Motivation for Using Distance Learning

I n the next four chapters the results of both the quantitative and qualitative research are described. In this chapter, general demographic data are presented, then compiled responses to questions are shown as they relate to the question of institutional motivation. In Chapter 7, specific administrative practices are detailed. In Chapter 8, indicators of the commercialization of higher education are examined. Chapter 9 then correlates variables connecting institutional motive to pedagogical approaches.

DEMOGRAPHIC DATA

With both the survey and the interviews, an attempt was made to contact the individual at specific institutions with the primary responsibility for distance learning programs. As one can see from Table 6.1, this effort was for the most part successful, with 78.1% reporting that they either do or may speak for their institution. The vast majority (81.0%) of respondents reported that they are classified as full-time administrators (see Table 6.2).

Surprisingly, the doctoral degree–granting institutions were a slight majority (32.0%), with community colleges (which usually dominate in responses to such surveys) representing less than a third (30.2%) of respondents (see Table 6.3).

When broken down by Carnegie classification for those institutions which could be identified, a larger percentage (39.6%) was found to be

Table 6.1
Do you speak for your institution? (Survey Question B)

Do you speak for your institution?

		Frequency	Percent	Valid Percent	Cumulative Percent
Valid	yes	101	57.4	58.0	58.0
	maybe	35	19.9	20.1	78.2
	no	38	21.6	21.8	100.0
	Total	174	98.9	100.0	
Missing	System	2	1.1		
Total		176	100.0		

Note: Numbers in most tables are rounded to nearest percentage.

Table 6.2
Position (Question 1)

Are you

		Frequency	Percent	Valid Percent	Cumulative Percent
Valid	full-time administrator	136	77.3	81.0	81.0
	part-time administrator	10	5.7	6.0	86.9
	tenured faculty	19	10.8	11.3	98.2
	part-time faculty	3	1.7	1.8	100.0
	Total	168	95.5	100.0	
Missing	System	8	4.5		
Total		176	100.0		

Table 6.3
Institutional Type (Question 2)

Highest degree your institution awards?

		Frequency	Percent	Valid Percent	Cumulative Percent
Valid	associate	52	29.5	30.2	30.2
	bachelor's	15	8.5	8.7	39.0
	master's	50	28.4	29.1	68.0
	doctorate	55	31.3	32.0	100.0
	Total	172	97.7	100.0	
Missing	System	4	2.3		
Total		176	100.0		

community college level (see Table 6.4). However, note here that 32 anonymous respondents were not identified by this scheme. The majority (78.8%) of respondents were from public institutions (see Table 6.5). When breaking out these Carnegie classified institutions by public or private responses from those completing the survey, it was found that the large majority (96.2%) of the associate's colleges and doctoral/research-extensive institutions (84.2%) who responded to the survey are public (see Table 6.6).

This sample from the higher education institutions most involved in distance learning showed a very large amount of activity, with over a 35.4% increase in the number of distance learning courses offered, from 9,826 in 1998–99 to 13,308 in 1999–2000. The mean average number of courses offered in 1999–2000 was 75.6 per institution. Table 6.7 gives a breakdown of

Table 6.4
Institutional Type, Carnegie Classification

type

		Frequency	Percent	Valid Percent	Cumulative Percent
Valid	Associate's Colleges	57	32.4	39.6	39.6
	Baccalaureate Colleges-Lib	1	.6	.7	40.3
	Baccalaureate Colleges-G	7	4.0	4.9	45.1
	Master's Colleges & UI	27	15.3	18.8	63.9
	Master's Colleges & UII	8	4.5	5.6	69.4
	Doctoral/Research-Ext	27	15.3	18.8	88.2
	Doctoral/Research-Int	4	2.3	2.8	91.0
	Specialized Institutions	13	7.4	9.0	100.0
	Total	144	81.8	100.0	
Missing	System	32	18.2		
Total		176	100.0		

Table 6.5
Public or Private Institution (Question 3)

Your institution is

		Frequency	Percent	Valid Percent	Cumulative Percent
Valid	public	134	76.1	78.8	78.8
	independent	36	20.5	21.2	100.0
	Total	170	96.6	100.0	
Missing	System	6	3.4		
Total		176	100.0		

Table 6.6
Public or Private Institution, Carnegie Classification (Question 3)

type * Your institution is Crosstabulation

Count

		Your institution is		Total
		public	independent	
type	Associate's Colleges	54	2	56
	Baccalaureate Colleges-Lib	1		1
	Baccalaureate Colleges-G	5	2	7
	Master's Colleges & UI	19	8	27
	Master's Colleges & UII	4	4	8
	Doctoral/Research-Ext	22	3	25
	Doctoral/Research-Int	2	2	4
	Specialized Institutions	2	10	12
Total		109	31	140

the number of courses offered by Carnegie classification. (Note: The difference in total number of courses offered between the preceding tables and Table 6.7 is accounted for by the 32 anonymous institutions who could not be classified by the Carnegie scheme.)

Many have noted the differences in approach, policies, and economics attached to the technologies used in distance learning courses (Bates, 2000; Jewett, 1999). As Table 6.8 shows, although the respondents are often involved in multiple technologies, Internet-based courses are clearly the most dominant form of delivery (49.7%).

EXPLICIT REASONS FOR USING DISTANCE LEARNING

The explicit reasons for using distance learning focused primarily on access—at 92.0% this was by far the most common reason for using distance learning. The second most common response was a belief in the pedagogical advantages of distance learning (62.5%), followed by a desire to keep up with the competition (55.1%). Table 6.9 shows the responses to the query about motives for use of distance learning. The "other" category showed a wide variety of responses, some emphasizing the broader categories listed in Table 6.9, others listing institution-specific factors (see Table 6.10).

When pressed further to give weight to specific possible motivations, access again was validated at a 90.7% rate of agreement (see Table 6.11). The pursuit of IT skills for students was of less interest, with 25.0% denying that this is a primary role for their institution at all (see Table 6.12). However, two-year (62.0%) and master's degree–granting (58.0%) institutions found

Table 6.7
Number of Courses by Carnegie Classification (Questions 4 & 5)

Case Summaries

type		Number of distance learning courses Summer 1999-Spring 2000	Number of distance learning format courses Summer 1998-Spring 1999?
Associate's Colleges	N	53	53
	Mean	68.3208	43.3396
	Sum	3621.00	2297.00
Baccalaureate Colleges-Lib	N	1	1
	Mean	91.0000	30.0000
	Sum	91.00	30.00
Baccalaureate Colleges-G	N	6	6
	Mean	28.5000	19.3333
	Sum	171.00	116.00
Master's Colleges & UI	N	27	27
	Mean	44.5926	30.1111
	Sum	1204.00	813.00
Master's Colleges & UII	N	7	7
	Mean	93.0000	79.2857
	Sum	651.00	555.00
Doctoral/Research-Ext	N	24	24
	Mean	114.1667	97.5417
	Sum	2740.00	2341.00
Doctoral/Research-Int	N	4	4
	Mean	53.7500	19.2500
	Sum	215.00	77.00
Specialized Institutions	N	13	13
	Mean	115.7692	101.3077
	Sum	1505.00	1317.00
Total	N	135	135
	Mean	75.5407	55.8963
	Sum	10198.00	7546.00

this factor to be more of a motive than other types of institutions (see Table 6.13). In testing the hypothesis further regarding a pursuit of additional sources of revenue, only 18.6% denied that this was a concern (see Table 6.14). Note here that this contradicts the apparent lack of concern about new revenue sources found in Table 6.9. Nevertheless, doctoral degree–granting institutions indicated that pursuing new sources of revenue was important more frequently than did other types of institutions. Doc-

Table 6.8
Primary Technology Used (Question 37)

Which of the following technologies is used as the primary form of delivery for your distance learning courses?

		Frequency	Percent	Valid Percent	Cumulative Percent
Valid	internet	85	48.3	49.7	49.7
	pre-packaged videotape (not live)	14	8.0	8.2	57.9
	live video (one-way or two-way)	27	15.3	15.8	73.7
	telephone (audio only)	2	1.1	1.2	74.9
	print-based	14	8.0	8.2	83.0
	other	29	16.5	17.0	100.0
	Total	171	97.2	100.0	
Missing	System	5	2.8		
Total		176	100.0		

Table 6.9
Motivation (Question 6)

Statistics

		Provide access to wider student population	Provide IT skills for students	New source of revenue	reduce expenses	belief in teaching/ learning advantages of DL	Desire to keep up with competition	OTHER
N	Valid	162	35	70	25	110	97	176
	Missing	14	141	106	151	66	79	0

toral degree–granting institutions responded "yes" 56.4% of the time when questioned whether or not the pursuit of new sources of revenue for the institution through new program development was a primary concern, while associate (40.0%), bachelor's (40.0%), and master's (44.0%) degree–granting institutions responded affirmatively at a much lower rate (see Table 6.15). Somewhat surprisingly, reducing expenses did not seem to be a concern for most institutions, as can be seen in that only 21.8% answered "yes" when asked whether or not a reduction of labor and facility costs was a primary focus in institutional planning (see Table 6.16). Almost 90% of the respondents saw technology as offering pedagogical advantages, and, consequently, one might conclude, as contributing to a motivation for use (see Table 6.17). Keeping up with the Joneses also seemed to be a major reason for the use of distance learning. As Table 6.18 shows, 73.1% responded

Table 6.10
Other Motivation (Question 6)

OTHER

		Frequency	Percent	Valid Percent	Cumulative Percent
Valid		143	81.3	81.3	81.3
	access	1	.6	.6	81.8
	access for non-traditional students	1	.6	.6	82.4
	access new markets	1	.6	.6	83.0
	accomodate student time	1	.6	.6	83.5
	allows institutional change	1	.6	.6	84.1
	audience	1	.6	.6	84.7
	convenience and flexibility	1	.6	.6	85.2
	convenience for students	1	.6	.6	85.8
	experiment with dl	1	.6	.6	86.4
	geographic distance of student	1	.6	.6	86.9
	grant	1	.6	.6	87.5
	ideal for working adult students	1	.6	.6	88.1
	increase enrollment	1	.6	.6	88.6
	it's all we do	1	.6	.6	89.2
	keep faculty up-to-date	1	.6	.6	89.8
	LAAP grant	1	.6	.6	90.3
	meet student needs	1	.6	.6	90.9
	military primary mkt.	1	.6	.6	91.5
	mission	1	.6	.6	92.0
	mission of the college	1	.6	.6	92.6
	mission of the university	1	.6	.6	93.2
	more flexible for students	1	.6	.6	93.7
	mostly rural service area	1	.6	.6	94.3
	new president brought in	1	.6	.6	94.9
	provide consistency in content	1	.6	.6	95.5
	provide wider exposure	1	.6	.6	96.0
	reach adults without residency	1	.6	.6	96.6
	rural community	1	.6	.6	97.2
	small pop., large geo. area	1	.6	.6	97.7
	space limitations	1	.6	.6	98.3
	student access	1	.6	.6	98.9
	student demand	1	.6	.6	99.4
	very rural with poor weather	1	.6	.6	100.0
	Total	176	100.0	100.0	

Table 6.11
Access as Part of Mission (Question 7)

Is providing greater access to student populations part of your institutional mission?

		Frequency	Percent	Valid Percent	Cumulative Percent
Valid	yes	156	88.6	90.7	90.7
	maybe	9	5.1	5.2	95.9
	no	7	4.0	4.1	100.0
	Total	172	97.7	100.0	
Missing	System	4	2.3		
Total		176	100.0		

Table 6.12
Providing IT Skills as Primary Role (Question 8)

Do you see providing information technology skills for students as a primary role for your institution?

		Frequency	Percent	Valid Percent	Cumulative Percent
Valid	yes	87	49.4	50.6	50.6
	maybe	42	23.9	24.4	75.0
	no	43	24.4	25.0	100.0
	Total	172	97.7	100.0	
Missing	System	4	2.3		
Total		176	100.0		

Table 6.13
Providing IT Skills by Institution Type (Questions 2 & 8)

Highest degree your institution awards? * Do you see providing information technology skills for students as a primary role for your institution? Crosstabulation

			Do you see providing information technology skills for students as a primary role for your institution?			
			yes	maybe	no	Total
Highest degree your institution awards?	associate	Count	31	12	7	50
		% within Highest degree your institution awards?	62.0%	24.0%	14.0%	100.0%
	bachelor's	Count	4	6	5	15
		% within Highest degree your institution awards?	26.7%	40.0%	33.3%	100.0%
	master's	Count	29	10	11	50
		% within Highest degree your institution awards?	58.0%	20.0%	22.0%	100.0%
	doctorate	Count	22	14	19	55
		% within Highest degree your institution awards?	40.0%	25.5%	34.5%	100.0%
Total		Count	86	42	42	170
		% within Highest degree your institution awards?	50.6%	24.7%	24.7%	100.0%

Table 6.14
New Revenue Primary Concern (Question 9)

Is the pursuit of new sources of revenue for the institution through new program development a primary concern?

		Frequency	Percent	Valid Percent	Cumulative Percent
Valid	yes	80	45.5	46.5	46.5
	maybe	60	34.1	34.9	81.4
	no	32	18.2	18.6	100.0
	Total	172	97.7	100.0	
Missing	System	4	2.3		
Total		176	100.0		

Table 6.15
New Revenue Concern by Institution Type (Questions 2 & 9)

Highest degree your institution awards? * Is the pursuit of new sources of revenue for the institution through new program development a primary concern? Crosstabulation

			Is the pursuit of new sources of revenue for the institution through new program development a primary concern?			
			yes	maybe	no	Total
Highest degree your institution awards?	associate	Count	20	20	10	50
		% within Highest degree your institution awards?	40.0%	40.0%	20.0%	100.0%
	bachelor's	Count	6	4	5	15
		% within Highest degree your institution awards?	40.0%	26.7%	33.3%	100.0%
	master's	Count	22	17	11	50
		% within Highest degree your institution awards?	44.0%	34.0%	22.0%	100.0%
	doctorate	Count	31	19	5	55
		% within Highest degree your institution awards?	56.4%	34.5%	9.1%	100.0%
Total		Count	79	60	31	170
		% within Highest degree your institution awards?	46.5%	35.3%	18.2%	100.0%

Table 6.16
Reduction of Costs Primary Concern (Question 10)

Is the reduction of labor and facility costs a primary focus in institutional planning?

		Frequency	Percent	Valid Percent	Cumulative Percent
Valid	yes	37	21.0	21.8	21.8
	maybe	45	25.6	26.5	48.2
	no	88	50.0	51.8	100.0
	Total	170	96.6	100.0	
Missing	System	6	3.4		
Total		176	100.0		

Table 6.17
Belief in Teaching/Learning Advantages (Question 11)

Do you believe that technology offers specific teaching/learning advantages?

		Frequency	Percent	Valid Percent	Cumulative Percent
Valid	yes	153	86.9	89.5	89.5
	maybe	17	9.7	9.9	99.4
	no	1	.6	.6	100.0
	Total	171	97.2	100.0	
Missing	System	5	2.8		
Total		176	100.0		

Table 6.18
Necessary to Keep Up with Competition (Question 12)

Is it necessary to offer distance learning format courses in order to keep up with competing institutions?

		Frequency	Percent	Valid Percent	Cumulative Percent
Valid	yes	125	71.0	73.1	73.1
	maybe	30	17.0	17.5	90.6
	no	16	9.1	9.4	100.0
	Total	171	97.2	100.0	
Missing	System	5	2.8		
Total		176	100.0		

"yes" when asked whether it is necessary to offer distance learning format courses to keep up with competing institutions.

Time and again in this study, institutional representatives indicated access as a primary reason for involvement in distance learning. This issue of access is consistently an important one for community colleges. Note in particular the following excerpts from interviews discussing the different populations served (in response to question 4).

> The initial reason was much as it is today, to reach a population that was difficult to reach. We are a community college and we have a lot of older students, students who are disabled, married students with young children—that was our initial market for our telecourses. Students would only have to come to campus a couple times per semester. . . . We added our two-way video classroom to specifically reach those at our Delano Center. Those students are mostly Hispanic and are low social-economic level. For many of them 35 miles is just impossible. We also can't staff full-time instructors up there either. So our solution

was the two-way video classroom. (Greg Chamberlain, Dean of Learning Resources, Bakersfield College)

Again it is a matter of serving the student who needs education, degrees, or proficiencies. (Thornton Perry, Director of Distance Education, Bellevue Community College)

Here's the view from a regional comprehensive institution showing a concern similar to that expressed by the community colleges for providing access to the local geographical population. Notice here how the dean discusses the access motivation with faculty.

We've had distance learning for well over twenty years via interactive television, and it was started as a way of serving the rural, outstate population. At the same time, they developed the self-paced correspondence type courses. And again that was to serve the rural, adult, part-time student and give them access to our institution. . . . We are a regional comprehensive institution, and my argument would be that in order to serve our region we have to use distance education. That's certainly how I approach the faculty. We do it to increase access to our institution. I think the faculty look at it partly that way, but also that the part-time adult learner needs a variety of ways of coming in contact with the knowledge base of the institution. (John Burgeson, Dean of Continuing Education, St. Cloud State University)

A historically black college and university (HBCU) also emphasized access.

Access is definitely one of the reasons for our involvement in distance learning. We believe that for every one student who comes to [institution], another one would have but for the distance involved. (Faculty member and program director from HBCU)

Independent institutions also mention access, particularly to geographically remote students. However, it is interesting to see at one university how the initially stated desire to serve local geographically remote students has apparently led to expansion into additional states.

We felt that this was a wonderful opportunity to offer a quality master's degree program to those who wanted it but could not drive to our campus. I'm not familiar enough with the terrain of California to know if you have a lot of small, remote cities, but we do in Texas. We're a massive state, and there are a lot of pockets where there is not a university offering masters' to teachers within a hundred or two hundred miles. So we felt that we wanted to do something for those teachers in those areas. Subsequently, we went to six other states, so now we are offering

> this program in seven states. (Joy Edwards, Director of Graduate
> Studies, Texas Wesleyan University)

Some others have found the motivation a matter of technological opportunity, particularly with the rise of the Internet, allowing less expensive,
asynchronous communication.

> I think the reason for involvement is much like any other institution;
> the technology was evolving, the ability to do things asynchronously
> was evolving. Our faculty and students do not want to be left behind.
> (Carole Hayes, Coordinator, External Relations and Development,
> Office for Distributed and Distance Learning, Florida State Univer-
> sity)

Many institutions just seemed to stumble into distance learning, primarily moved by institutional leaders, both administrators and faculty, with an
interest in distance learning. Notice in this first interview how isolated the
development appears to have been, with little campus-wide discussion.

> I think he [the president] just saw it and wanted to do it. Nassau Com-
> munity College was involved in distance learning through the State
> University of New York. There was a program called the State Univer-
> sity of the Air, and we were part of that program. This just must have
> struck his fancy when he saw it, and [he] said, "we'll do it." There was-
> n't any institutional discussion as far as I know. (Arthur Friedman, Co-
> ordinator, College of the Air, Nassau Community College)
>
> Going back to the mid-1980s we had an academic dean who felt
> that essentially they [distance learning courses] were a good idea. And
> he proselytized this on campus and had the general support of the ad-
> ministration. (Thornton Perry, Director of Distance Education, Belle-
> vue Community College)
>
> The growth of our online program was faculty-driven, presi-
> dent-driven, and then student-driven. There has been a great deal of
> interest from students, classes close fast, and there are long waiting
> lists. (Vivian Sinou, Dean, Distance and Mediated Learning, Foothill
> College)
>
> Let's go back to the late 1970s. It was a very ad hoc kind of thing.
> You may remember the *Roots* television series; it was a dramatization
> based on the Alex Haley book. Somebody in the administration
> thought that this might be a good way to connect with the commu-
> nity, and they made an independent study course. People could sign up
> for credit if they wanted. There was a reading list. We had an instruc-
> tor. There were class sessions as the series continued. So that was liter-
> ally our first television course. It wasn't connected to anything other
> than somebody had an idea. Some of the faculty objected to that, even
> though the credit and course work at very best might transfer as an

> elective. (Thornton Perry, Director of Distance Education, Bellevue
> Community College)
>
> We offered our first course in 1994 or '95. The driving force was a
> computer science faculty member, Michael Loceff, who was in the
> forefront of technology and asked the president if he could offer one of
> his courses via email. That's how it all began. (Vivian Sinou, Dean,
> Distance and Mediated Learning, Foothill College)

In the following interview (and others), one can see the important role
leading research institutions have had in inspiring others to utilize distance
learning.

> Our president at that time went to a meeting at Stanford and saw what
> they were doing with the ITFS system. He came back here and decided
> that we ought to be doing that. And that's what started it. There was-
> n't any kind of grass roots effort, it was really the president. (Vice-Pres-
> ident, large, independent, urban, eastern U.S. doctoral
> degree–granting institution)

One institution pointed to the need to distinguish itself from others by
the use of distance learning and technology.

> What happened was that there was a new president and new dean of
> continuing education, and they had decided that one of the things this
> campus could do was distance learning, and compete with the other
> campuses in the CSU [California State University]. We were never
> going to have a blue pyramid [California State University, Long
> Beach] or Arabian horses [California State Polytechnic University,
> Pomona]; those things just weren't in the cards for us, but distance
> learning was something this campus could do without a huge invest-
> ment. (Warren Ashley, Director, Center for Mediated Instruction and
> Distance Learning, CSU Dominguez Hills)

Institutional survival was also described in one instance as a reason for
using distance learning. This passage is particularly interesting because it
reveals that while community colleges may not focus on seeking new
sources of revenue in the same way as independent institutions, they do
seek sustained enrollment for institutional survival.

> Online education for them will be the difference between being able
> to run the college or folding in the long run. Their economy was based
> on the military there, the China Lake military research facility, which
> has been downsizing. They are literally in the middle of the desert. So
> if they were going to survive as an institution, they literally had to look
> for other students. (Greg Chamberlain, Dean of Learning Resources,
> Bakersfield College)

Fear of being left behind in the use of technology for institutions also surfaced, particularly for four-year institutions seeing the widespread and highly publicized growth of distance learning in community colleges.

> The community colleges were aggressive in the development of distance learning, and the universities became concerned about being behind in the distance learning game. People were talking about the evolution of the academy and the end of the university, as we know it, and it's had an effect on the administration. (Carole Hayes, Coordinator, External Relations and Development, Office for Distributed and Distance Learning, Florida State University)

A related motivation has to do with the desire to improve national rankings through measurements of technology. One can see here that at one independent institution, this issue is particularly important.

> The first is that measures of quality institutions, one measure particularly in the *U.S. News and Report*, has to do with the techno-literacy of the faculty and the programs. Not having any online courses puts us low in that category; having online courses puts us higher in that category. I wouldn't want to think that that's what drives the whole thing, but it would be naïve to think that it doesn't have something to do with it. (Don Cardinal, faculty member, Chapman University)

The pursuit of new sources of revenue was identified as one reason by respondents. In this case, one can see that the Dean of Continuing Education is specifically identified as holding this view, as opposed to an academic department.

> The Dean of Continuing Education . . . thought that here's a way to develop new programs, generate revenue, and support other activities. Which was true. She was willing to invest money into it, whether I needed more lights, cameras, computers, whatever. Generally, it was true. It depends on where they put the revenue. . . . Generally they show us as losing money, but our programs make money. (Warren Ashley, Director, Center for Mediated Instruction and Distance Learning, CSU Dominguez Hills)

In contrast, many specifically deny that they are pursuing distance learning for money-making reasons. However, in the following responses one can see that the economics of distance learning appear somewhat muddy.

> I don't think that was a reason, and only recently has that become an issue in this. I think people are beginning to stand their ground a little bit. Flexibility is always an issue, especially at an institution as old as ours. So as you try to do new things, the money needs to come from somewhere else. You need to make a business plan that ultimately

shows that you are going to make money, or break even, and hopefully put some money back into other kinds of programs. (Vice-President, large, independent, urban, eastern U.S. doctoral degree–granting institution)

No, I don't think so. In fact throughout my experience, distance education was self-funded. We had to drum up enough students for these courses. The faculty teaching the courses were moonlighting, a fourth course [added to] the three that they normally taught. We've been kind of like a small business. As time has gone on we've been incorporated in the larger campus fiscal apparatus. (Thornton Perry, Director of Distance Education, Bellevue Community College)

In our particular district, we are going to continue to see online education as a way to reach our constituency and meet their needs. We're not going to go for. . . . Foothill-DeAnza has this thing with Japan, we don't see it as a moneymaker. (Greg Chamberlain, Dean of Learning Resources, Bakersfield College)

More indirectly, in answer to the question about pursuit of new revenue sources, some see distance learning as a marketing tool to attract new students to the institution.

Frankly, it feeds students into traditional programs. If you have a student taking courses at a distance, they can become interested in taking courses at the campus, and that is always available to them. It introduces them to the people, the process on campus. They are part of that culture. So it's a good marketing tool for the main campus, and it's a major growth area for the university as a whole. (Vice-President, large, independent, urban, eastern U.S. doctoral degree–granting institution)

If you look at it from the overall university perspective, distance learning is an excellent way of reaching students we would not ordinarily reach. These students are limited by time and location and would have difficulty attending classes on our campus. Our university administration does not see us as a threat to on-campus enrollment, but instead, as an alternative for students who cannot attend class on-campus. Our on-campus enrollments and distance education enrollments continue to increase. (Allan Guenther, Marketing Coordinator for Distance Education, The University of Alabama)

From an institutional side, it is partly motivated by marketing, that is, this will increase our student base. (Jon Raibley, Assistant Director of Lifelong Learning Center, Western Seminary)

A more practical motivation to deal with limited space issues was mentioned at one community college.

Over the next five years in terms of growth, where we want to be, there is no way we could get there physically in terms of facilities. Now our

> only room for growth is virtual. The only space to grow is virtual. We
> don't have any room for classrooms. (Dean, representative from com-
> munity college)

Some institutions also see one of their roles as keeping their students
up-to-date with technological changes.

> There is a belief in higher education that technology belongs to us to
> some degree. That we are supposed to be teaching technology to
> young people, and teaching an online course is not only a pedagogical
> issue. And actually that jury is still out, but there is a functional issue. I
> want my students to take my online course even if it's a push pedagogi-
> cally, because I want them to have the skills that it took for them to do
> that. . . . When we asked the question if undergraduates should have
> laptops, the question wasn't only if they should have laptops, but are
> we keeping up with the Joneses? Are we maximizing technology for
> learning? So I think that's the institutional motivation. (Don Cardi-
> nal, faculty member, Chapman University)

One community college described the way they have defined themselves as
a high technology institution.

> It [technology] has become part of the college ethos, and online
> courses and distance ed[ucation] are simply a part of that. (Thornton
> Perry, Director of Distance Education, Bellevue Community College)

In looking for data relevant to the academic capitalism inquiry, responses from a few of the research institutions give an indication of a direct
relationship between distance learning and the pursuit of corporate relationships. Particularly for a few of the research institutions interviewed, a
specific desire to increase ties with industry became clear (in response to
question 9).

> [We are] a little different than most schools because our largest per-
> centage of students are our graduate students, and that means much of
> what we do is linked to the corporate community. And this was a way
> of strengthening that link, and creating some new links. (Vice-Presi-
> dent, large, independent, urban, eastern U.S. doctoral degree–grant-
> ing institution)
>
> What I can say is that [our university] has many relationships with
> industry and these are very important, particularly to the School of
> Engineering. A lot of engineering needs interaction with industry for
> research verification, and many other reasons including being able to
> serve in different ways many different industries' needs. There is a
> long, long history here at [our university]. You don't think of [our uni-
> versity] as being associated with industry, or even manufacturing,

where I used to be, yet there are long-term relationships among faculty, departments, and industry particularly around research, research centers, and particularly here with distance education. (Program Manager, independent, western U.S. doctoral degree–granting institution)

The program started in 1992 under the direction our chairman at the time, Professor Peter. Z. Bulkeley. He felt it was important for the department to have a direct tie to industry. One of the ways the department could accomplish this was through the development of a distance learning program using videoconferencing technology. (Elizabeth Spencer-Dawes, Distance Learning Administrator, Boston University)

The belief that there are pedagogical advantages to the use of technology was also an expressed motivation.

There might even be some more noble reasons that have a lesser influence, such as the belief that there is a pedagogical advantage. That's certainly my motivation. The other things are there, I have to admit, but my personal measure is: is learning greater for my students with technology, or without it? (Don Cardinal, faculty member, Chapman University)

A number of faculty got interested, primarily because they saw online teaching as a way to stay current, challenged, and be rejuvenated with new teaching methods. (Vivian Sinou, Dean, Distance and Mediated Learning, Foothill College)

INSTITUTIONAL NARRATIVE HISTORIES

One strategy used in the interviews was to inquire about the history of distance learning use with an eye toward revealing indirect motivation in the various narrative accounts (question 5). One narrative describes how distance learning was used to increase enrollments in a stalled program.

Of course when the Internet came along, we never say no. We had this B.A. in science limping along. . . . So here came the Internet, and it seemed too obvious to me that we need more people to draw from. This was not the degree for everyone, but it is for some. So we put it on the Internet in 1995. . . . So we went online in 1995 with the first complete degree program, certainly the first in the CSU [California State University], one of the first nationally. That program today has more than 300 [students] worldwide. (Warren Ashley, Director, Center for Mediated Instruction and Distance Learning, CSU Dominguez Hills)

A typical pattern seen in the narrative history of many of the institutions was a growth of distance learning programs coinciding with the development of new technologies. From these accounts one can see that in some ways the new technology is driving the distance learning programming.

> At Bakersfield College, we started in 1992 into telecourses. That was our first foray into distance learning. In 1996 we added a distance learning classroom, which is two-way audio and video, going to one of our remote centers about 35 miles away. All of these things we continue to do now. Our third modality in distance learning we started in the Fall of 1997, and that is the online distance courses. Enrollments in all of our [distance learning] programs have continued to grow. As of this year we have over 2,300 students. (Greg Chamberlain, Dean of Learning Resources, Bakersfield College)
>
> We've really just grown from that, from an ITFS system, to a satellite teleconferencing system, a production system so that now we are broadcasting on satellite, on cable systems, via microwave, via ITFS. And now we are not just a video production facility, we are getting involved in multimedia and many more things. We're putting video on CD and sending that out, we're creating Web sites to support the classes, we're getting involved in streaming audio and video, and actually getting involved in a number of international projects as well. (Vice-President, large, independent, urban, eastern U.S. doctoral degree–granting institution)
>
> Of course the first programs to start were the independent study, correspondence by mail programs. That program started 70 to 75 years ago, and is a well-established program. The distance education that people know of, with new technological advancements, began in 1991 when we launched the videotape program. That program began as one for engineering students for the military, others in the country, and around the world. That developed into a very large and successful program. Our online courses began in 1997. We also offer courses by satellite and videoconferencing. Those programs began after 1991. (Public Relations Director, large, public, southern U.S. doctoral degree–granting institution)

Other institutional histories reveal partnerships with for-profit groups and industry.

> Canter Educational Productions developed the video, or developed a couple of videos we used with our programs. Because of our long history with Canter Educational Productions they came to us and asked if we would be interested in developing future programs together in video. And we said that we would think about it. We thought about it,

and it took about at least a year for this older faculty to adjust to the idea that not all learning has to be done in a traditional setting with a faculty member and students in a classroom, four-by-four class: four walls, four corners of a book. We started a partnership with Canter five years ago and began with the courses they developed. And then we partnered with them in developing the other courses which would constitute the rest of the program. (Joy Edwards, Director of Graduate Studies, Texas Wesleyan University)

Research affiliations exist with the Fraunhofer Center for Manufacturing Innovation and United Technologies Corporation, among others. United Technologies is one industry group that works with us in distance learning. They also fund the United Technology Seminar Series held in our department on a weekly basis. There are additional projects, beyond the purview of the distance learning program but within the department, some of which are a result of the department working with companies through the distance learning program. (Elizabeth Spencer-Dawes, Distance Learning Administrator, Boston University)

For one institution, the narrative history reveals the way in which distance learning has been part of an overall focus on technology.

The college itself has become a focus of high technology. It's rather a convoluted situation, but the State of Washington provided the building, the college approaches both Boeing and Microsoft for significant funding, because they are the two significant movers and shakers here, and the whole focus is high technology. Utilization of the Web, computer programming. We have the Northwest Center for Emerging Technology, which has been working with the National Science Foundation on its second or third grant to develop education and technology. (Thornton Perry, Director of Distance Education, Bellevue Community College)

Many institutions describe how grants have played a role in the development of distance learning. Survey results show grants as a major force behind the original implementation of distance learning, with 45.9% responding "yes" to the question of whether the availability of funding sources encouraged the development of their distance learning programs (see Table 6.19). The narrative histories confirm the importance of grants and public funding for the development of distance learning programs.

In 1980, 1979, the school received a grant which allowed it to do videotaping and [it] produced 23 videotaped courses, and started an external program with those courses. (Jon Raibley, Assistant Director of Lifelong Learning Center, Western Seminary)

Table 6.19
Funding Sources Encouraging Development (Question 14)

Have the availability of funding sources and/or new state or federal government agencies encouraged the development of your distance learning programs?

		Frequency	Percent	Valid Percent	Cumulative Percent
Valid	yes	78	44.3	45.9	45.9
	maybe	29	16.5	17.1	62.9
	no	63	35.8	37.1	100.0
	Total	170	96.6	100.0	
Missing	System	6	3.4		
Total		176	100.0		

... it started with a $200,000 grant from E-college to develop these new programs online. So although some faculty had developed courses partially or completely online, this institutional-wide effort was started with the grant. (Faculty and Program Director, HBCU)

MISSION

The question of motivation in the surveys and interviews was also probed by querying the respondents on how they see distance learning fitting with the overall institutional mission (interview question 10). Almost all (91.8%) indicated in survey responses that distance learning was consistent with their institutional mission; only 2 of 171 respondents to this question said "no" (see Table 6.20). When analyzed by institutional type (see Table 6.21) we see that doctoral degree–granting institutions responded "yes" at a slightly higher rate (94.5%) than two-year institutions (88.0%). The interviews also reveal that some institutions find the fit between distance learning and their mission very easy.

> I think it fits quite nicely with our mission. While we are quite traditional, there is a notion among comprehensive institutions that not only do they serve the daytime student that can come to campus, but also ... serve the local community and the region. We are after all a regional institution. And I think it's pretty true that institutions during the sixties and seventies tried to reach out and serve a broader regional audience, rather than just the traditional student. (John Burgeson, Dean of Continuing Education, St. Cloud State University)
> It fits in nicely with the mission of trying to be all things to all people. That's not what the mission states, but it is what it boils down to. To provide as many avenues, or portals to use a buzzword, to access the

Table 6.20
Consistent with Institutional Mission (Question 22)

Do you feel that the distance learning program is consistent with your institutional mission?

		Frequency	Percent	Valid Percent	Cumulative Percent
Valid	yes	157	89.2	91.8	91.8
	maybe	12	6.8	7.0	98.8
	no	2	1.1	1.2	100.0
	Total	171	97.2	100.0	
Missing	System	5	2.8		
Total		176	100.0		

Table 6.21
Consistent with Institutional Mission by Type (Question 22)

Highest degree your institution awards? * Do you feel that the distance learning program is consistent with your institutional mission? Crosstabulation

			Do you feel that the distance learning program is consistent with your institutional mission?			Total
			yes	maybe	no	
Highest degree your institution awards?	associate	Count	44	5	1	50
		% within Highest degree your institution awards?	88.0%	10.0%	2.0%	100.0%
	bachelor's	Count	14	1		15
		% within Highest degree your institution awards?	93.3%	6.7%		100.0%
	master's	Count	45	4		49
		% within Highest degree your institution awards?	91.8%	8.2%		100.0%
	doctorate	Count	52	2	1	55
		% within Highest degree your institution awards?	94.5%	3.6%	1.8%	100.0%
Total		Count	155	12	2	169
		% within Highest degree your institution awards?	91.7%	7.1%	1.2%	100.0%

education they need. (Thornton Perry, Director of Distance Education, Bellevue Community College)

I see it fitting in terms of providing an education for anyone, for audiences that can get here, or have trouble getting here. (Coordinator, large, public, southern U.S. doctoral degree–granting institution)

Many of the respondents to the mailed survey were specialized religious institutions, confirming the suggestion in the literature review that there is a very long history of religious institutional involvement in various forms of nontraditional and distant learning. A specialized religious institution describes how distance learning fits with its mission:

> From the mission point of view, we have wanted to train for the ministry internationally but haven't been able to do that. Now we can. What that means is that we are more practical than we have been in the past. If we have to take a pastor from his ministry and bring him here to Portland, Oregon, and train for two or three years, and then send them back or to a new job, then we've lost two years of them being able to do their work. And then broken relationships and all sorts of things. So distance ed[ucation] allows them to train at a distance and apply it to their job. (Jon Raibley, Assistant Director of Lifelong Learning Center, Western Seminary)

Some institutions have even incorporated distance learning into their formal missions.

> One of [the] things the president wanted to do was rewrite the mission statement, and distance learning is in it. There's a commitment to make distance learning convenient and accessible to people, which is what distance learning is all about. (Warren Ashley, Director, Center for Mediated Instruction and Distance Learning, CSU Dominguez Hills)
>
> Saybrook has always been a distance education institution. Being a distance education institution allows people from all over the world to continue the important work they are doing, wherever it is that they live, while participating in humanistic and transpersonal dialogue and study at Saybrook. The work that they do vocationally often feeds into the work they do scholastically at Saybrook. (Kathy Wiebe, Admissions Coordinator, quoting Mindy Myers, V. P. Recruitment and Admissions, Saybrook Institute)

Some public institutions see their mission applying only to their geographical areas, which defines them and limits their notion of distance learning. We see here that this viewpoint differentiates them from independent institutions.

> Most of our students live within 15 miles of the institution. What we've tried to do is keep it close to their work, their families, and their education. So we've kept it relatively close. We are attracting students from our county, from New York City, and the county to our east, Suffolk County. We haven't gone past that area because of our mission. (Arthur Friedman, Coordinator, College of the Air, Nassau Community College)
>
> I just came back from the Massey Center, which is a kind of a think tank on distance learning, in Orlando, and there were 3,500 people

there. And I'd say 85% were from the corporate world and they are all getting into distance learning, or e-learning as they call it. They don't have nearly the experience we have, and you see them heading in directions you know are wrong, and you realize that you have a tremendous advantage over them because you have the accreditation and degrees, and none of them can do that. So if we do this right, we can be wonderfully successful. . . . State organizations and institutions are limited by their very charters to geographical areas and beyond that it is hard to get funding, and that just doesn't work in this new world. So we've got an advantage there. (Vice-President, large, independent, urban, eastern U.S. doctoral degree–granting institution)

One can see from the data presented in this chapter that institutional motivation for the use of distance learning is a very complex topic, one that emphasizes the great variety and diversity of American higher education. While the pursuit of new sources of revenue is a factor in motivating institutions to use distance learning, it is clearly not the only one. In Chapter 10 some conclusions will be drawn from the data presented in this chapter. In the next chapter, data relevant to the administrative practices of distance learning in higher education are examined.

CHAPTER

Administrative Practices

I n this chapter I focus on specific distance learning administrative practices such as administrative structure, course development, and assessment.

WHO INITIATED THE USE OF DISTANCE LEARNING?

Another indicator of institutional motivation and a way of understanding
how an institution regards distance learning is to see who began the process. While one can see from the survey data in Table 7.1 that top administrators (32.2%) most often began the push for implementation, faculty
members (22.2%) and the continuing education department (26.3%) also
played large roles. When broken out by institutional type (see Table 7.2)
we see that continuing education divisions were involved in initiation
more at doctoral degree-granting institutions (44.4%), while top administrators were most commonly responsible at two-year (38.0%) and master's
degree–granting (42.0%) institutions.

ADMINISTRATIVE STRUCTURE

An important indicator in understanding an institution's motivations and
their ramifications lies in where the staff performing distance learning
functions are housed. Generally, the administrative structure of distance

Table 7.1
Who Initiated Distance Learning (Question 13)

Who initiated the use of distance learning courses at your institution?

		Frequency	Percent	Valid Percent	Cumulative Percent
Valid	top administrators	55	31.3	32.2	32.2
	continuing education	45	25.6	26.3	58.5
	individual faculty	38	21.6	22.2	80.7
	task force/committee	12	6.8	7.0	87.7
	external agency	1	.6	.6	88.3
	other	20	11.4	11.7	100.0
	Total	171	97.2	100.0	
Missing	System	5	2.8		
Total		176	100.0		

Table 7.2
Who Initiated Distance Learning by Institutional Type (Questions 2 & 13)

Highest degree your institution awards? * Who initiated the use of distance learning courses at your institution? Crosstabulation

			Who initiated the use of distance learning courses at your institution?						
			top administrators	continuing education	individual faculty	task force/committee	external agency	other	Total
Highest degree your institution awards?	associate	Count	19	3	13	9		6	50
		% within Highest degree your institution awards?	38.0%	6.0%	26.0%	18.0%		12.0%	100.0%
	bachelor's	Count	1	3	6	1		4	15
		% within Highest degree your institution awards?	6.7%	20.0%	40.0%	6.7%		26.7%	100.0%
	master's	Count	21	13	9	2		5	50
		% within Highest degree your institution awards?	42.0%	26.0%	18.0%	4.0%		10.0%	100.0%
	doctorate	Count	14	24	10		1	5	54
		% within Highest degree your institution awards?	25.9%	44.4%	18.5%		1.9%	9.3%	100.0%
Total		Count	55	43	38	12	1	20	169
		% within Highest degree your institution awards?	32.5%	25.4%	22.5%	7.1%	.6%	11.8%	100.0%

learning tends toward either an academic or service notion of administration. In the survey, respondents indicated the following when asked in what administrative unit the distance learning program is housed.

Category	n	valid %
Continuing Education	59	42.5%
Academic Afairs	23	16.5%
Distance Learning	21	15.1%
Academic Department	21	15.1%
Computing Services	15	10.8%

In the interviews, those identifying themselves as academic units either report to academic affairs or to a specific academic department (question 6).

> Continuing education is part of Academic Affairs, and I report to a dean and then a VP of Academic Affairs. (Warren Ashley, Director, Center for Mediated Instruction and Distance Learning, CSU Dominguez Hills)
>
> It's under Education, because this is the only distance learning we have. (Joy Edwards, Director of Graduate Studies, Texas Wesleyan University)
>
> I have a coordination function. . . . We're under the office of the Vice President for Academic Affairs. (Arthur Friedman, Coordinator, College of the Air, Nassau Community College)
>
> We are part of the School of Engineering. The number of courses we offer are engineering, but we could approach other schools and departments. (Program Manager, independent, western U.S. doctoral degree–granting institution)
>
> I am under the School of Business. (Faculty and Program Director, HBCU)

Others report to an extended education/continuing education division, or are seen as a service unit under an administrative service banner.

> I am [a] member of the College of Continuing Studies, one of the colleges here. In Continuing Studies there are five different divisions, and distance education is one of them. (Allan Guenther, Marketing Coordinator for Distance Education, the University of Alabama)
>
> . . . the office I am in is called the Office for Distributed and Distance Learning. This office reports to the Vice President for Program Development and Faculty Support. So we are not part of any academic unit but are a service unit. (Carole Hayes, Coordinator, External Relations and Development, Office for Distributed and Distance Learning, Florida State University)
>
> I'm under an associate dean of telecommunications who in turn reports to two deans: the executive dean and the dean of technology. So we have a separate deanship that deals only with technological matters. (Thornton Perry, Director of Distance Education, Bellevue Community College)
>
> Division of Distance and Distributed Learning. Out of the Office of Public Service. (Vice-President, large, independent, urban, eastern U.S. doctoral degree–granting institution)
>
> I work closely with faculty (over 70) and division deans. Online faculty don't report to me, but I support them with the delivery, design, and management of their online classes. Let's say a faculty member

wants to offer a course online, how do I go about that? How do I order textbooks? How can I get assistance to examine my course pedagogically? (Vivian Sinou, Dean, Distance and Mediated Learning, Foothill College)

ACADEMIC OVERSIGHT

Academic oversight for distance learning is generally seen as paralleling usual processes. About three-quarters of the respondents report this to be the case, while 23.2% indicate that the process is different (see Table 7.3). When broken down by institutional type we find that only 11.3% of the doctoral degree–granting institutions responded that they have a different course approval process, while two-year institutions responded at a rate of 34.7% to the same question, and master's degree–granting institutions responded affirmatively 24.5% of the time (see Table 7.4). The interviews confirm the survey data and explain further the specific institutional process (question 8).

> They are considered right along with the other courses. (Coordinator, large, public, southern U.S. doctoral degree–granting institution)
>
> . . . it's done in the way that ordinary courses are handled. (Elizabeth Spencer-Dawes, Distance Learning Administrator, Boston University)
>
> In terms of approvals, it goes through the department and the division. If for instance a lit instructor wants to put something online that they've been doing, it goes to the chair of the department, the division. Then it comes to us over here [in Distance Education], and if I have any questions I go back to the department or division. When the course is approved, funds are accrued for the development of the course. . . . If it's a new course, say in science fiction, they'd have to go through the process. But in terms of how it's delivered, it's not really a factor. Only the fact that it is a new course, that heretofore had not

Table 7.3
Academic Approval (Question 19)

Does your institution have a different procedure for the academic approval of distance learning format courses?

		Frequency	Percent	Valid Percent	Cumulative Percent
Valid	yes	39	22.2	23.2	23.2
	no	129	73.3	76.8	100.0
	Total	168	95.5	100.0	
Missing	System	8	4.5		
Total		176	100.0		

Table 7.4
Academic Approval by Institutional Type (Questions 2 & 19)

Highest degree your institution awards? * Does your institution have a different procedure for the academic approval of distance learning format courses? Crosstabulation

| | | | Does your institution have a different procedure for the academic approval of distance learning format courses? | | Total |
			yes	no	
Highest degree your institution awards?	associate	Count	17	32	49
		% within Highest degree your institution awards?	34.7%	65.3%	100.0%
	bachelor's	Count	4	11	15
		% within Highest degree your institution awards?	26.7%	73.3%	100.0%
	master's	Count	12	37	49
		% within Highest degree your institution awards?	24.5%	75.5%	100.0%
	doctorate	Count	6	47	53
		% within Highest degree your institution awards?	11.3%	88.7%	100.0%
Total		Count	39	127	166
		% within Highest degree your institution awards?	23.5%	76.5%	100.0%

been offered. (Thornton Perry, Director of Distance Education, Bellevue Community College)

The graduate faculty oversee the distance learning program, just as they do with the regular graduate courses. As with all programs, the graduate programs are under the oversight of a campus-wide Graduate Program Committee, and then that committee is overseen by the Academic Affairs Committee. That is a campus-wide committee responsible for oversight of all academic issues at the university. (Joy Edwards, Director of Graduate Studies, Texas Wesleyan University)

To the extent that the course needed further university approval, for a regular course or broadcast, then they would do that. [For] a new program needing approval, they would normally do that. So, it's not separate from the normal academic process. (Vice-President, large, independent, urban, eastern U.S. doctoral degree–granting institution)

Some institutions do not develop new course content for distance learning delivery, but only offer distance learning courses which are the same as traditional courses. This undoubtedly simplifies the course approval process.

Just like regular courses, they need to be accredited. It's not a whole lot different; the course needs to be basically the same as a course offered here on campus. (Manager, doctoral degree–granting institution)

The mechanism we use is the Curriculum Committee, for approval of an existing course, and we are accredited by the Southern Association of Colleges and Schools and follow all of their guidelines. When a previously approved course is augmented or converted to an online course, there is a form that must be filled out and approved by the department, the College, and the faculty curriculum committee before it can go on and be offered. . . . What you are indicating with the form is that this course has been previously approved, and you are enhancing the course or revising the way it is being taught. What the form says is that your peers have looked at the changes in the course and approve and recognize that the course has been appropriately augmented and that the course is as good or better than the originally approved course. It usually goes faster than the original approval process. (Carole Hayes, Coordinator, External Relations and Development, Office for Distributed and Distance Learning, Florida State University)

Some respondents indicated that approval was primarily an academic department matter.

Courses or programs that the Division of Distance Education offers must first be approved by the individual department that houses the course or program. (Allan Guenther, Marketing Coordinator for Distance Education, the University of Alabama)

. . . they go to their division or department, and then to the curriculum committee like for any other course. Then the faculty member is directed to us for help with the development, planning, and delivery of the course. If anything gets stopped, it usually gets stopped at the division or department level where some faculty are not as open to distance learning. (Vivian Sinou, Dean, Distance and Mediated Learning, Foothill College)

However, some institutions have implemented additional policies and requirements for distance learning oversight, or are now considering changes.

I think we are still in a place where we need more oversight than a traditional course. (Don Cardinal, faculty member, Chapman University)

If more than 50% of the program is distance learning, then it needs approval at the school level. It's called "substantive change." (Warren Ashley, Director, Center for Mediated Instruction and Distance Learning, CSU Dominguez Hills)

One of the things we've found with our new courses is that our model that we are using for distance education is getting more scrutiny from the faculty than any course on campus would ever receive. And that's a good thing. We keep telling ourselves that it is a good thing because it will keep us holding what we do to the highest standard. We can go to accrediting agencies and say we've developed these courses carefully, here's our proof. (Jon Raibley, Assistant Director of Lifelong Learning Center, Western Seminary)

We started by saying that any course should have the same content, the same rigor no matter how it is delivered. Therefore, we make no distinction on transcripts, for example. If you take Math D it doesn't matter if you took it in the learning lab, if you took it online. What we basically have on our curriculum sheet is an extra check box, delivered in other modalities. This will be delivered online, etc. I think we are going to have to change that. I don't know if you are aware of it, but WASC [Western Association of Schools and Colleges] right now is looking at guidelines for the delivery of courses and degrees through electronic delivery methods. We are in the process right now of looking at that document and thinking, maybe we need to do this a little differently. (Greg Chamberlain, Dean of Learning Resources, Bakersfield College)

One respondent described what is undoubtedly a common experience as part of the process of approving distance learning, with various campus committees questioning whether they might have jurisdiction.

So the departments must certify that any distance learning course we offer is congruent with any course we offer on campus. It requires departmental approval and notification to the campus-wide committee that it is the same. There are a number of campus committees that have taken a part in looking at distance learning. . . . We have a pretty extensive assessment program, and they have looked at it. The college-wide curriculum committee has assumed some responsibility, and has asked for a report on distance learning. The college resources committee believes it has some purview as well, because it uses academic resources. But there isn't really any one committee to take this on. The curriculum committee tried to take overall control, but didn't [succeed]. (Arthur Friedman, Coordinator, College of the Air, Nassau Community College)

COURSE DEVELOPMENT

Course development is revealing as an administrative procedure because it shows who controls the process. In response to the survey question about who decides who teaches a distance learning course, it was found that the majority of the decision-making was controlled either by the academic department (34.3%) or jointly with faculty members and administrators (30.4%).

Academic department: 34.3%

Joint decision between faculty and administrator: 30.4%

Faculty: 21.9%

Distance education director: 13.4%

An additional aspect of the course development process is the degree to which the courses are developed by individuals or by teams. Primarily, courses seemed to be developed by individuals (54.7%), and to a lesser extent by a combination of both teams and individuals (37.6%). Very few institutions develop all courses through teams only (7.6%). (See Table 7.5.) When analyzed by institutional type we see that doctoral degree–granting institutions responded at a slightly higher rate (13.0%) than master's degree-granting (6.1%) and two-year institutions (4.0%) that they develop courses with teams (see Table 7.6).

However, this is clearly complicated. Often interviewees seem to indicate that the control in the process flows back and forth, or is joint. Accordingly, many of the interviewees who responded to this question focused on the faculty-driven and academic department control of course development (question 17).

> Most of the time, the faculty came to us with an idea, and mostly it was faculty who knew about a population that could be served. They knew about a need. For example, we have quite a few courses in our applied psychology area because they were actively trying to recruit students from an area south of here. (John Burgeson, Dean of Continuing Education, St. Cloud State University)

Table 7.5
Course Development (Question 34)

Are courses typically developed by faculty/instructors through

		Frequency	Percent	Valid Percent	Cumulative Percent
Valid	teams	13	7.4	7.6	7.6
	individuals	93	52.8	54.7	62.4
	both	64	36.4	37.6	100.0
	Total	170	96.6	100.0	
Missing	System	6	3.4		
Total		176	100.0		

Table 7.6
Course Development by Institutional Type (Questions 2 & 34)

Highest degree your institution awards? * Are courses typically developed by faculty/instructors through Crosstabulation

			Are courses typically developed by faculty/instructors through			
			teams	individuals	both	Total
Highest degree your institution awards?	associate	Count	2	26	22	50
		% within Highest degree your institution awards?	4.0%	52.0%	44.0%	100.0%
	bachelor's	Count	1	7	6	14
		% within Highest degree your institution awards?	7.1%	50.0%	42.9%	100.0%
	master's	Count	3	31	15	49
		% within Highest degree your institution awards?	6.1%	63.3%	30.6%	100.0%
	doctorate	Count	7	28	19	54
		% within Highest degree your institution awards?	13.0%	51.9%	35.2%	100.0%
Total		Count	13	92	62	167
		% within Highest degree your institution awards?	7.8%	55.1%	37.1%	100.0%

It's been faculty-driven. We started by saying, "Any of you faculty interested?" And we had stipends for the first semester for developing new courses. We have not had stipends since, and interestingly enough, we have not had many new courses developed since. I wonder if there's a correlation there? We also tapped our technologically savvy, wanting-to-jump-in people. (Greg Chamberlain, Dean of Learning Resources, Bakersfield College)

We do not develop courses specifically for distance learning. We are basically going into [institution] courses. (Manager, independent doctoral degree–granting institution)

The way they [faculty] design their class is the way it's going to be. I can sit up here and tell them to use streaming video and chat rooms, but sometimes they just want to stick to good ol' email. (Coordinator, large, public, southern U.S. doctoral degree–granting institution)

The courses we offer to distance learning students are identical to those offered on campus. There is no difference, except that not all on-campus courses are offered through the distance learning program. If a faculty member is willing to teach their course to distance learning students, the program adopts the course. (Elizabeth Spencer-Dawes, Distance Learning Administrator, Boston University)

Other interview subjects indicated that administration and market forces have influence over the development process.

I've hired someone whose responsibility is to develop new distance learning programs. She meets regularly with departments to try and add new video, Internet, and self-paced courses. She's been pretty successful at this. (John Burgeson, Dean of Continuing Education, St. Cloud State University)

We're currently looking at this program and saying, "Where are we going with this?" We're looking at a couple of programs such as biotech[nology]. (Greg Chamberlain, Dean of Learning Resources, Bakersfield College)

Some note that development occurs in a combination of ways.

It was ad hoc. (Thornton Perry, Director of Distance Education, Bellevue Community College)

My sense is that the videotape courses were developed by interested faculty first. We have a course here, a faculty member here, let's videotape it. Now we are coming from a planned perspective, thinking about what we want and then developing the courses for the certificate program, and then contact the faculty member. (Jon Raibley, Assistant Director of Lifelong Learning Center, Western Seminary)

We do distance learning here, but there are other parts of the university that are also involved. Each department decides if it wants to do distance learning, and they may have their own technical person. They may come to us and we can consult to help them. Whether it is videoconferencing or WebCT, we help them set it up. So in many cases there is distance learning going on that we may not be aware of because the other departments are doing their thing, and have the means. A lot of my frustration is that students will call with problems, and we don't know about the course. (Coordinator, large, public, southern U.S. doctoral degree–granting institution)

They are developed in two ways: first, through my office, the Office of Distant and Distributed Learning, we develop new courses in an organized fashion, and then secondly, individual faculty members are encouraged to develop their own courses using technology to enhance their courses. (Carole Hayes, Coordinator, External Relations and Development, Office for Distributed and Distance Learning, Florida State University)

Haphazard. Many of the courses are developed from faculty who had radio shows on our station and started to get involved by preparing lectures for the radio station. Most of the things we do on the radio station are prerecorded to fit the time slots, so we can use the programs over and over again. (Arthur Friedman, Coordinator, College of the Air, Nassau Community College)

A combination of things. We do encourage faculty to develop certain courses based on the interest level of our students. Increasingly, faculty members are developing their courses online and allowing the Division of Distance Education to market the courses. Then there are other courses that are developed in a team manner whereby the faculty member and the Division of Distance Education work together to develop an online course. The Division of Distance Education Web team assists in the course creation process. Then there is the other extreme where a faculty member says, "Here are my notes, make a course out of them." So we really have all three versions of development. (Allan Guenther, Marketing Coordinator for Distance Education, the University of Alabama)

ASSESSMENT PRACTICES

The way administrative units assess student learning is an important part of academic oversight. Additionally, assessment reveals how much an institution concerns itself with authenticating student work. In the survey responses, we see that the vast majority (88.3%) either sometimes or always use proctored tests in their distance learning format courses (see Table 7.7). When broken down by institutional type we find that master's degree–granting institutions responded that they use proctored tests less often in distance learning courses (12.2% "always") in comparison to two-year institutions (28.0% "always") and doctoral degree–granting institutions (25.5% "always") (see Table 7.8).

The interviews further establish that many of the institutions rely on proctored tests (question 18).

They are required to have proctored tests. (John Burgeson, Dean of Continuing Education, St. Cloud State University)

Many of the instructors do use midterms and finals. Many use a proctoring system. We have a proctoring system where an online student can identify a clergy person, a local librarian, a principal to proctor the test. The test is then mailed to the proctor, the proctor administers the test and mails it back. (Greg Chamberlain, Dean of Learning Resources, Bakersfield College)

Table 7.7
Proctored Tests (Question 35)

Do you generally require a proctored test for course completion?

		Frequency	Percent	Valid Percent	Cumulative Percent
Valid	always	39	22.2	22.8	22.8
	sometimes	112	63.6	65.5	88.3
	never	20	11.4	11.7	100.0
	Total	171	97.2	100.0	
Missing	System	5	2.8		
Total		176	100.0		

Table 7.8
Proctored Tests by Institutional Type (Questions 2 & 35)

Highest degree your institution awards? * Do you generally require a proctored test for course completion? Crosstabulation

			Do you generally require a proctored test for course completion?			Total
			always	sometimes	never	
Highest degree your institution awards?	associate	Count	14	30	6	50
		% within Highest degree your institution awards?	28.0%	60.0%	12.0%	100.0%
	bachelor's	Count	4	10		14
		% within Highest degree your institution awards?	28.6%	71.4%		100.0%
	master's	Count	6	33	10	49
		% within Highest degree your institution awards?	12.2%	67.3%	20.4%	100.0%
	doctorate	Count	14	37	4	55
		% within Highest degree your institution awards?	25.5%	67.3%	7.3%	100.0%
Total		Count	38	110	20	168
		% within Highest degree your institution awards?	22.6%	65.5%	11.9%	100.0%

All our courses have proctored tests, but it may be at a mutually agreed upon site and it doesn't involve the faculty member. For example, the testing site may be at a military base in another part of the world, or it may be here on the university campus. (Allan Guenther, Marketing Coordinator for Distance Education, the University of Alabama)

Yes, we have proctored tests. At United Technologies we have a proctor on site that manages that. We have site coordinators that manage individual sites. If it is a non–United Technologies student I'll contact them, and often we will use an alum at that site that is not taking classes. Often HR will designate someone to work with. (Elizabeth Spencer-Dawes, Distance Learning Administrator, Boston University)

Yes, in the School of Business we require at least one proctored exam either on campus or at a center near them. (Faculty and Program Director, HBCU)

Some require proctored exams. Students don't necessarily need to come to our campus; they can go to a testing center at another community college closer to them. (Vivian Sinou, Dean, Distance and Mediated Learning, Foothill College)

From the responses of some of the interviewees one can see the great effort and difficulty involved in administering proctored tests.

For the undergraduate level, by and large it is proctored testing. Some discipline areas have made good arguments against proctored testing, and so in some instances there isn't proctored testing. But that goes back to part of what I was hired to do, and that was to make agreements with the community colleges around the state to provide proctored testing as well as other support services. Of the 28 community colleges in Florida, 18 of them contract with us to provide support services to students in their area. (Carole Hayes, Coordinator, External Relations and Development, Office for Distributed and Distance Learning, Florida State University)

Others stress the similarities to traditional classroom practices in approach to assessment.

One of the things we've always stressed is that the program on campus should be the same as the one used in distance learning. Whatever assessment is used should be the same. (Warren Ashley, Director, Center for Mediated Instruction and Distance Learning, CSU Dominguez Hills)

The students are in a [institution] course and are evaluated as any other student in the course would be evaluated. (Manager, independent doctoral degree–granting institution)

Some are careful in their approach to instructional design, making it impractical for students to cheat.

What I do is work with instructors on course design, on pedagogy, on instructional design. The bottom line is that if I have 200 people in my psych course, I don't know if that's really Mary. I've never asked Mary for an ID. If I teach that online course like the psych course, yes, I'm going to have problems. But if you teach it as it should be taught and you have readings this week, and you have to respond, be in the discussion group three times a week, and do all of these little steps, then we head more towards portfolio assessment. If you are going to get somebody to do all that work all along for you, that's a little different than getting someone to go and take the midterm and final for you. (Greg Chamberlain, Dean of Learning Resources, Bakersfield College)

No, we don't require it. One of the things we've learned is that faculty can get to know the students well in the online environment, they know if they are the ones taking the test or writing the assessment. Writing styles become very familiar. (Carole Hayes, Coordinator, External Relations and Development, Office for Distributed and Distance Learning, Florida State University)

Others use timed online tests and software to combat plagiarism.

The old argument, how do you know it is Sally Smith taking the course? Instructors have tried to build timed assignments into their courses. If it's a timed test it precludes students from looking up all the answers. We subscribe to a service called plagarism.org [now Turnitin.com] wherein we can check to see if the work is the student's or someone else's. (Thornton Perry, Director of Distance Education, Bellevue Community College)

One respondent reported using a more qualitative measure of portfolio assessment.

No, we have written work sent to the faculty. At the end of the program they must [have] presented a portfolio to a faculty. They add pieces as they go along so that by the end they have a full portfolio. (Joy Edwards, Director of Graduate Studies, Texas Wesleyan University)

Another institution described program evaluation using student surveys and interviews.

Student performance is one way to assess, but we also do surveys and extensive interviews. (Coordinator, large, public, southern U.S. doctoral degree–granting institution)

Some admit to the problems in their system and the difficulties involved.

That has been a weakness. We are looking for a better assessment tool. We've tried a few different things, but we are still looking for a good, objective, assessment tool. (Jon Raibley, Assistant Director of Lifelong Learning Center, Western Seminary)

The data on distance learning administrative practices show that top administrators and the continuing education department led more than half of the distance learning efforts (58.5%), and that distance learning is more often housed in continuing education and distance learning administrative units (57.6%). Nevertheless, it was generally found that key administrative practices such as course approvals, course development, and assessment parallel traditional practices. The next chapter examines the commercialization of higher education through the use of distance learning.

CHAPTER

Commercialization Indicators

In this chapter I look for indications of the commercialization of higher education through the use of distance learning. When considering distance learning as an example of higher education's commercialization, the pattern of faculty compensation inevitably emerges as a central aspect. Compensation indicators include direct and indirect forms of compensation (as discussed earlier in Chapter 4). In terms of direct compensation, the use of part-time faculty, compensation for teaching, and compensation for course development are key indicators of the commercialization of higher education. For indirect compensation, intellectual property rights, training, and recognition are also indicators of this trend. Other commercialization indicators examined in the chapter include management approaches, partnerships with for-profit entities, administrative innovations, and budgets. Additionally, the specific influence of revenue-seeking institutional motive on practices is evaluated. Finally, interviewees reflect on the change process and emerging faculty roles prompted by the rise of distance learning.

USE OF PART-TIME FACULTY

The use of part-time faculty is a commonly raised issue in addressing the degree to which institutions implement distance learning as an attempt to increase their revenue. We saw earlier that one way distance learning can reduce expenses is by substituting less expensive part-time faculty for full-time faculty. However, the survey results show that most institutions are predominantly using full-time faculty rather than adjuncts (see Table 8.1).

This is an important and somewhat surprising result. In trying to understand these surprising data, it is useful to consider the results from the Primary Research Group study (1999), which found an increased use of part-time faculty from 1998 to 1999. In that study, the authors surmised that full-time faculty had been used to develop and teach new distance learning courses at first, but then later on had been replaced by part-time faculty. Therefore it is possible that the low use of adjunct faculty thus far is a result of the early stage of development of distance learning programs. Given the controversial nature of distance learning, it makes sense that administrators would turn to full-time faculty rather than adjunct to develop and teach courses at the beginning when they are under the most scrutiny.

In general, there are no great differences by type of institution, as seen in Table 8.2. Thus, all types report that three-quarters or so of the distance learning courses are not taught by adjuncts, ranging from 72.9% at the two-year institutions up to 85.7% at the baccalaureate colleges. Conversely, the proportion of institutions who use adjuncts to teach half or more of their distance learning courses falls within a small range: 8.4% of the two-year colleges to 14.3% of the baccalaureate colleges. In summary, it is clear that all institution types are primarily using regular faculty to teach distance learning courses at this time. (Note: The difference in count totals between here and later crosstabulations is a result of some institutions reporting on only one of the variables crosstabulated.)

Those interviewed mostly indicated that they rely on regular faculty (question 11).

Table 8.1
Adjunct Faculty Use (Question 31)

What is the percentage of faculty teaching distance learning courses that are classified as adjunct faculty?

		Frequency	Percent	Valid Percent	Cumulative Percent
Valid	0-25	128	72.7	76.6	76.6
	26-50	20	11.4	12.0	88.6
	51-75	7	4.0	4.2	92.8
	76+	12	6.8	7.2	100.0
	Total	167	94.9	100.0	
Missing	System	9	5.1		
Total		176	100.0		

Table 8.2
Adjunct Faculty Use by Institutional Type (Questions 2 & 31)

Highest degree your institution awards? * What is the percentage of faculty teaching distance learning courses that are classified as adjunct faculty? Crosstabulation

			What is the percentage of faculty teaching distance learning courses that are classified as adjunct faculty?				Total
			0-25	26-50	51-75	76+	
Highest degree your institution awards?	associate	Count	35	9	3	1	48
		% within Highest degree your institution awards?	72.9%	18.8%	6.3%	2.1%	100.0%
	bachelor's	Count	12			2	14
		% within Highest degree your institution awards?	85.7%			14.3%	100.0%
	master's	Count	39	4	2	5	50
		% within Highest degree your institution awards?	78.0%	8.0%	4.0%	10.0%	100.0%
	doctorate	Count	40	7	1	4	52
		% within Highest degree your institution awards?	76.9%	13.5%	1.9%	7.7%	100.0%
Total		Count	126	20	6	12	164
		% within Highest degree your institution awards?	76.8%	12.2%	3.7%	7.3%	100.0%

Exclusively regular faculty to develop the courses. (Manager, independent, doctoral degree–granting institution)

It is 99% tenured faculty on campus. In the interactive television we may have some we call fixed term or adjunct faculty. Some adjunct. By and large, it is tenured members of the faculty. (John Burgeson, Dean of Continuing Education, St. Cloud State University)

Yes, these are all regular faculty. The courses are the same as taught on campus, the only difference is the mode of delivery. (Faculty and Program Director, HBCU)

One community college representative indicates that the wide use of full-time faculty is not a requirement, but a matter of availability.

The majority are full-time faculty, but we do have part-time faculty teaching in each of the modalities. There is nothing that says we have to use full-time faculty, or part-time faculty, it is just a matter of who is available in a department to teach. (Greg Chamberlain, Dean of Learning Resources, Bakersfield College)

Some report using a combination of both full-time and part-time faculty.

Both. More and more regular full-time faculty have gotten involved. Early on it was more part-timers. (Thornton Perry, Director of Distance Education, Bellevue Community College)

A combination of both. Most of the faculty that teach online and video courses are full-time professors here on campus. But we do have some part-time. Most of the high school courses that we offer through written correspondence are graded by instructors who work full time in the Tuscaloosa city and county school systems. (Allan Guenther,

Marketing Coordinator for Distance Education, the University of Alabama)

Most are regular faculty, but we do have adjunct faculty teaching two of our operations management courses. Also, we have a faculty member from the School of Management teaching an operations management course, by agreement with the School. (Elizabeth Spencer-Dawes, Distance Learning Administrator, Boston University)

One interviewee reported the greater use of adjunct faculty.

Most are adjunct. We do currently have three full-time faculty teaching, but most are taught by adjunct faculty. (Joy Edwards, Director of Graduate Studies, Texas Wesleyan University)

At a specialized religious institution, the interviewee indicated that they are considering moving to the use of adjunct faculty.

We have been using our regular faculty, but are now contemplating using adjunct faculty. (Jon Raibley, Assistant Director of Lifelong Learning Center, Western Seminary)

COMPENSATION

The most apparent characteristic of compensation patterns found in this study is their striking irregularity. However, as Table 8.3 shows, the majority are paid as regular load with normal enrollment limits (37.3%). Agreements for compensation as regular load with no ceiling on enrollment (6.0%), and regular load with additional pay after seat maximum (3.6%), when combined with the previous general regular load figure, total almost half of the responses (46.9%). On the key question of payment of a stipend for teaching distance learning courses, only 14.5% reported such a practice. The granting of additional preparation time (9.0%) and payment on an overload basis (9.6%) were less commonly reported by respondents. Only 4.2% of the respondents report not using full-time faculty at all. Additionally, there seems to be little difference in compensation for the various technologies and delivery platforms, with 79.0% of those responding reporting that they do not compensate faculty any differently in using different technologies for the delivery of distance learning (see Table 8.4).

One can see in Table 8.5 that community colleges tend to compensate faculty more through regular load payment (47.9% regular load with normal enrollment limits, compared to 32.1% for doctoral degree–granting institutions), and are less likely to pay an additional stipend (8.3% compared to 18.9% for doctoral degree–granting institutions). Master's de-

Table 8.3
Faculty Compensation (Question 24)

How are full-time faculty compensated for teaching distance learning format courses?

		Frequency	Percent	Valid Percent	Cumulative Percent
Valid	regular load with normal enrollment limits	62	35.2	37.3	37.3
	regular load with no ceiling on enrollment	10	5.7	6.0	43.4
	regular load with additional pay after seat maximum	6	3.4	3.6	47.0
	with additional preparation time	15	8.5	9.0	56.0
	on overload basis	16	9.1	9.6	65.7
	additional stipend	24	13.6	14.5	80.1
	regular load for in-person class, per head for remote stu.	5	2.8	3.0	83.1
	other	21	11.9	12.7	95.8
	do not use full-time faculty	7	4.0	4.2	100.0
	Total	166	94.3	100.0	
Missing	System	10	5.7		
Total		176	100.0		

Table 8.4
Faculty Compensation and Specific Technology (Question 25)

Are faculty compensated differently for different types of technologies utilized?

		Frequency	Percent	Valid Percent	Cumulative Percent
Valid	yes	35	19.9	21.0	21.0
	no	132	75.0	79.0	100.0
	Total	167	94.9	100.0	
Missing	System	9	5.1		
Total		176	100.0		

gree–granting institutions reported a slightly higher affirmative response to the question of *not* using full-time faculty (4.1% as opposed to 1.9% in doctoral degree–granting institutions and 2.1% in two-year institutions).

The interviews show that within some institutions there are differences among academic units as to their compensation policies, often leaving decisions up to academic departments (question 11).

> Regarding load, it is done on an individual basis. Some are on full load already, and we work with the academic dean to make it part of their load. Others on a full load, we pay them on a stipend basis. We con-

Table 8.5
Faculty Compensation by Institutional Type (Questions 2 & 24)

Highest degree your institution awards? * How are full-time faculty compensated for teaching distance learning format courses? Crosstabulation

		How are full-time faculty compensated for teaching distance learning format courses?									Total
		regular load with normal enrollment limits	regular load with no ceiling on enrollment	regular load with additional pay after seat maximum	with additional preparation time	on overload basis	additional stipend	regular load for in-person class, per head for remote studen	other	do not use full-time faculty	
Highest degree your institution awards? associate	Count	23	3	2	5	5	4		5	1	48
	% within Highest degree your institution awards?	47.9%	6.3%	4.2%	10.4%	10.4%	8.3%		10.4%	2.1%	100.0%
bachelor's	Count	5		2			1	1	2	3	14
	% within Highest degree your institution awards?	35.7%		14.3%			7.1%	7.1%	14.3%	21.4%	100.0%
master's	Count	17	4	1	5	4	8	1	7	2	49
	% within Highest degree your institution awards?	34.7%	8.2%	2.0%	10.2%	8.2%	16.3%	2.0%	14.3%	4.1%	100.0%
doctorate	Count	17	3	1	5	7	10	2	7	1	53
	% within Highest degree your institution awards?	32.1%	5.7%	1.9%	9.4%	13.2%	18.9%	3.8%	13.2%	1.9%	100.0%
Total	Count	62	10	6	15	16	23	4	21	7	164
	% within Highest degree your institution awards?	37.8%	6.1%	3.7%	9.1%	9.8%	14.0%	2.4%	12.8%	4.3%	100.0%

tract with them to develop their courses for additional compensation. (Jon Raibley, Assistant Director of Lifelong Learning Center, Western Seminary)

    That's been negotiated on an individual program basis. (Carole Hayes, Coordinator, External Relations and Development, Office for Distributed and Distance Learning, Florida State University)

    [Compensation] probably varies from department to department. (Public Relations Director, large, public, southern U.S. doctoral degree–granting institution)

An HBCU representative spoke about the differences in compensation based on enrollment expectations by subject matter.

    It is done differently depending on the department. In Business we expect the courses to be large, so there is a rationale for overload payment. (Faculty and Program Director, HBCU)

Some institutions have labor agreements that specify rates of pay and what are not considered as part of load.

    We are under a collective bargaining agreement that defines load and overload in very specific ways and does not include what we term "packaged courses." The contract defines what we pay on those courses, which is $[amount] per student. It also stipulates what we pay for interactive television, which is based on a credit [basis]—it is not part of load. (John Burgeson, Dean of Continuing Education, St. Cloud State University)

Some institutions do consider teaching distance learning courses as part of regular faculty load, with or without extra compensation for course development.

    Yes, part of their load. (Joy Edwards, Director of Graduate Studies, Texas Wesleyan University)

    It is considered as part of their load, but they are compensated with a stipend for developing a course and receive a fee per student. There is a way of compensating the instructor for the extra workload. (Vice-President, large, independent, urban, eastern U.S. doctoral degree–granting institution)

    It's regular load when they are teaching, because they have so many assistants, the mentors. For developing the two plus two online courses, faculty get a two-course release stipend. So if their usual load is three courses, they would teach one and then the support for the other two would be developing the online course. When they do that they have the assistance of our Web staff, technical editors, instructional design people, graphics people, all of those sorts of things. We have a project manager to make sure things move along. (Carole

Hayes, Coordinator, External Relations and Development, Office for
Distributed and Distance Learning, Florida State University)

One respondent indicated concern over the university faculty compensation policy.

They get paid as with any other course. There is no additional pay,
which concerns me. (Coordinator, large, public, southern U.S. doctoral degree–granting institution)

Some of those interviewed do offer some sort of stipend for course development.

Not contractually, but generally we have to pay because that's generally how you get someone to do something new. (John Burgeson, Dean
of Continuing Education, St. Cloud State University)

They are all paid a stipend for course development, and the load
question is still being sorted out. (Faculty and Program Director,
HBCU)

Yes, they do tend to get an additional incentive for teaching a distance learning course, in addition to their regular salary. (Elizabeth
Spencer-Dawes, Distance Learning Administrator, Boston University)

INTELLECTUAL COPYRIGHT

Another key issue in understanding the revenue motivation for institutions is who owns the intellectual copyright to distance learning format
courses. The survey shows that almost half (46.4%) of respondents view
the courses as the property of the institution. In only a small number of instances (16.1%) does institutional policy clearly give intellectual property
interests exclusively to the faculty member. A middle ground of joint institution and faculty ownership is occupied by 17.9% of the respondents.
Those indicating that they are still struggling with the formation of a policy
represent a surprisingly small 10.7% (see Table 8.6).

However, a comparison of copyright policy by type of institution (see
Table 8.7) shows that two-year community colleges (63.3%) and the small
number of institutions offering bachelor's degrees (78.6%) are much more
likely to respond that the institution itself holds the rights (master's degree–granting institutions report 30.6%; doctoral degree–granting institutions report only 34.0%). Conversely, doctoral degree–granting (26.4%)
and master's degree–granting institutions (16.3%) are more likely to respond that faculty own the rights to the courses they develop (as opposed to
10.2% for two-year institutions). Joint ownership was claimed at a much

Table 8.6
Intellectual Property Rights (Question 30)

When a full-time faculty member develops a distance learning course as part of either regular load, overload, or for a stipend, who owns the intellectual property rights?

		Frequency	Percent	Valid Percent	Cumulative Percent
Valid	faculty	27	15.3	16.1	16.1
	institution	78	44.3	46.4	62.5
	joint	30	17.0	17.9	80.4
	no policy	18	10.2	10.7	91.1
	other	13	7.4	7.7	98.8
	do not use	2	1.1	1.2	100.0
	Total	168	95.5	100.0	
Missing	System	8	4.5		
Total		176	100.0		

higher rate at master's degree-granting institutions (30.6%) than at either community colleges (14.3%) or doctoral degree–granting institutions (13.2%). (Note: Here again there is a discrepancy in the total responses between figures due to those respondents who did not answer both crosstabulated questions.)

In general, the interviews show a great deal of confusion and lack of clear policy on intellectual copyright (question 11). Some have no policy or are only now considering a policy.

> (laughs) You are asking about some pretty serious stuff, my friend. I think because we [the department] are only five years new, this hasn't been worked out. As more faculty become involved, this will become more of an issue. . . . To answer your question, they get no extra compensation, and if they leave the university there is no policy on whether or not they can take it with them. (Coordinator, large, public, Southern U.S. doctoral degree–granting institution)
>
> No, we haven't dealt with anything like that. (Joy Edwards, Director of Graduate Studies, Texas Wesleyan University)

One community college representative expressed discomfort over using a retired faculty member's course materials.

> Since we license most of the courses, this isn't an issue. That's an issue we have to face. I'd like to get at department-created materials, so that it's not a problem [using retired faculty's materials when they leave the institution]. We did have a course we had to stop because the faculty had retired, and I didn't feel it was appropriate to pick that up. (Arthur

Table 8.7
Intellectual Property Rights by Institution Type (Questions 2 & 30)

Highest degree your institution awards? * When a full-time faculty member develops a distance learning course as part of either regular load, overload, or for a stipend, who owns the intellectual property rights? Crosstabulation

			When a full-time faculty member develops a distance learning course as part of either regular load, overload, or for a stipend, who owns the intellectual property rights?						Total
			faculty	institution	joint	no policy	other	do not use	
Highest degree your institution awards?	associate	Count	5	31	7	5	1		49
		% within Highest degree your institution awards?	10.2%	63.3%	14.3%	10.2%	2.0%		100.0%
	bachelor's	Count		11	1	1	1		14
		% within Highest degree your institution awards?		78.6%	7.1%	7.1%	7.1%		100.0%
	master's	Count	8	15	15	6	3	2	49
		% within Highest degree your institution awards?	16.3%	30.6%	30.6%	12.2%	6.1%	4.1%	100.0%
	doctorate	Count	14	18	7	6	8		53
		% within Highest degree your institution awards?	26.4%	34.0%	13.2%	11.3%	15.1%		100.0%
Total		Count	27	75	30	18	13	2	165
		% within Highest degree your institution awards?	16.4%	45.5%	18.2%	10.9%	7.9%	1.2%	100.0%

Friedman, Coordinator, College of the Air, Nassau Community College)

Others have clear policies that show if a faculty member is paid for course development, then the institution owns the course in a work-for-hire arrangement.

If a faculty develops a course, there is an option of two-ninths release time, two courses a term. Or an equivalent additional pay which comes to about $[amount]. They can make their course. If they accept this stipend, then the course belongs to the college, it's mounted on the college's server, we use a WebCT platform. (Thornton Perry, Director of Distance Education, Bellevue Community College)

Everything developed for distance learning courses is the property of Boston University. At the University's TLTR, we have discussed the issues surrounding intellectual property though to my knowledge we have not adopted a policy on the issue. (Elizabeth Spencer-Dawes, Distance Learning Administrator, Boston University)

Saybrook [Institute] owns the courses. (Kathy Wiebe, Admissions Coordinator, Saybrook Institute)

One administrator indicated that the institution owns the course under a work-for-hire arrangement, but that subsequent royalty arrangements are negotiated separately.

Basically it is looked at as work for hire, because people are being paid to do this work. Now if products are developed and are licensed from this, the provost will negotiate with the faculty member for copyright. Royalties, ownership, are negotiated on a case-by-case basis. (Carole Hayes, Coordinator, External Relations and Development, Office for Distributed and Distance Learning, Florida State University)

Some have developed licensing agreements with faculty.

It's interesting. We don't really have an institutional policy right now. . . . What we are doing now is licensing the course for three years from the faculty even when we pay to have it developed. After three years, if we are interested then we can re-license. That's what was suggested to me by a copyright attorney, and I've heard this suggested at various conferences I've attended. Rather than haggling over copyright, it is easier just to license the material. (John Burgeson, Dean of Continuing Education, St. Cloud State University)

Many of those interviewed expressed a general approach of maintaining the status quo.

No, we have some vague language in the contract. . . . The bottom line is that we treat it just like any other course. You can have my course outline, my syllabus. If [I] have a Web page you can have that, but everything that I've collected in the filing cabinet in my office is mine to take with me. Now that's informal, but basically that's the way we're operating right now. (Greg Chamberlain, Dean of Learning Resources, Bakersfield College)

We have said that the content is the faculty member's. We don't lay claim to that. However, the format is the property of the school. (Jon Raibley, Assistant Director of Lifelong Learning Center, Western Seminary)

Yes, the decision hasn't been finalized, but the committee set up to review this is recommending that the faculty retain ownership, but that the university can use the course for two years after a faculty member leaves. (Faculty and Program Director, HBCU)

Some commented on faculty attitudes toward the issue.

Yeah, the legal department is very aware of this issue. My unit, which started distance learning here, mostly came from a broadcasting background and were very concerned with this issue. We haven't had any problems. Initially, the only problem came from the faculty who were concerned that their materials would be ripped off from them. (Vice-President, large, independent, urban, eastern U.S. doctoral degree–granting institution)

I think copyright issues are always of concern to faculty, and it depends on person-to-person [relationships] how they relate to that. (Manager, independent, doctoral degree–granting institution)

CORPORATE MANAGEMENT APPROACHES

To better ascertain the degree to which distance learning administrative practices are changing the university—leading it toward more of a corporate approach—interviewees were questioned about some of their practices and general organizational philosophy (question 6). Many of those interviewed indicated a preference for more entrepreneurial or market-driven approaches to education.

So I was brought on, and a large part of my task was to see what we could do with distance learning. So we started to look at all the options and possibilities, and in the process we developed a reputation of never saying no. No matter what someone proposed, we'd say yes. (Warren Ashley, Director, Center for Mediated Instruction and Distance Learning, CSU Dominguez Hills)

New program development is one area where interview subjects revealed market approaches to their management of distance learning.

> Then the thing was what are we going to do about programming? Because I don't think we can be all things to all people. And so we started to look at things, and my approach was always to look at a market and find what no one else is doing, and sew up that market. That's my idea of competing, to play on a field where there is no one else. And usually that's what we did. Even today the only program that we have that is the same as what other people have is the M.B.A. . . . And I told them that it was a bad idea, the world doesn't need another distance learning M.B.A. It just doesn't need it. But our people wanted to do it and our School of Management runs that on their own. All the other programs we have are unique. We have a degree in quality assurance, a master's in conflict management, we are the only ones in the country that have that. We have an M.A. in humanities through correspondence, and that continues to exist. We have the first B.S.N. out there. Now there's hundreds. I'm not real excited about that. (Warren Ashley, Director, Center for Mediated Instruction and Distance Learning, CSU Dominguez Hills)

One interview subject focused on custom, on-site training as an approach to serving specific markets.

> The new school will use market research to see where there is demand. At that point we go to the faculty to see if they have the content, and if they do we will work with them to turn it into another format. . . . For example, we are doing contract work for, let's say, project management, and it's made specifically for them. . . . I really think that we need to get to the point where we almost customize every degree. (Vice-President, large, independent, urban, eastern U.S. doctoral degree–granting institution)

This programming concern was especially focused on the corporate market for the following interview subjects.

> We are getting feedback that some course content is too theoretical and not directly applicable to the work of engineers in industry. Consequently, we have refocused the M.S. degree coursework in the area of technical product leadership to coincide with the move in industrial companies to integrate their design and manufacturing activities. (Elizabeth Spencer-Dawes, Distance Learning Administrator, Boston University)
>
> Obviously, if there were strong needs in industry, we would bring that to their attention. But it's up to the faculty and the department to

decide. (Program Manager, independent, western U.S. doctoral degree–granting institution)

Often in the interviews a shift to an emphasis on student needs was apparent. Some might connect a focus on student needs with a market-driven
approach to higher education.

> In our case, although we have some students from out of the state and
> out of the country, the majority of our students live in our county. Now
> we have a huge county. But the majority of the students are taking
> these courses to avoid commuting, time shifting, and so on. (Greg
> Chamberlain, Dean of Learning Resources, Bakersfield College)
>
> So you're making things more convenient, minimizing commuting
> time.... Eighty-five to ninety percent of the distance ed students are
> local, and most of those are also enrolled in traditional classes. What
> they are trying to do is mix and match a schedule so they can proceed
> towards a degree at a normal pace, and still fit other things in. (Thorn-
> ton Perry, Director of Distance Education, Bellevue Community Col-
> lege)
>
> The largest group of our online students are working adults who
> can't get to campus a certain number of days a week to attend classes,
> or moms who can only study at night when the kids are asleep. Com-
> muting is a big problem in the Bay Area. Some of our online students
> would rather take a face-to-face class, but take it online because they
> can save time from having to commute. (Vivian Sinou, Dean, Dis-
> tance and Mediated Learning, Foothill College)
>
> The median age is 34. Most work full-time and have families. Most
> are motivated to improve job skills or change what they do. (Coordi-
> nator, large, public, southern U.S. doctoral degree–granting institu-
> tion)

The following institutions made the argument that distance learning is
serving to develop new markets, particularly adult learners and those currently employed in industry.

> These are graduate students aimed at a new market and they are not
> from our traditional student base. (Faculty and Program Director,
> HBCU)
>
> They are all working in industry. (Elizabeth Spencer-Dawes, Dis-
> tance Learning Administrator, Boston University)

One institution noted the market advantage of traditional universities offering distance learning courses over new providers entering the marketplace.

A lot of students don't mind taking distance learning courses, but they want to know they're taking it from a real institution, that there are real bricks and mortar behind it someplace. And if they want to they can come to the campus and visit and know that they are a part of it. (Allan Guenther, Marketing Coordinator for Distance Education, the University of Alabama)

CORPORATE PARTNERSHIPS

One important indicator of higher education's commercialization is the formation of partnerships with for-profit entities. The interviews suggest that most of the interaction with corporations had to do with the licensing of software (question 9).

We are experimenting with a company called Smarthinking that provides online tutoring. We're looking at WebCT. . . . Faculty this semester and next are playing with these tools that companies are providing to us free, and then next year we will make some decisions. (Greg Chamberlain, Dean of Learning Resources, Bakersfield College)

The licenses we have now are for software such as Blackboard. We don't license any complete courses. (Coordinator, large, public, southern U.S. doctoral degree–granting institution)

Many replied that they have not entered into such agreements with for-profit entities for various reasons.

We have not done that as of yet. I guess in the tradition of the brick and mortar university, it's going to take time to do something like that. We're taking baby steps. (Allan Guenther, Marketing Coordinator for Distance Education, the University of Alabama)

We haven't at this point. We talked to E-College, but because we have WebCT we haven't made that decision yet. A number of other institutions have tried to get us to put our courses on their Web sites; I'm always getting letters like that. . . . Haven't had a need for for-profit partnerships. (Arthur Friedman, Coordinator, College of the Air, Nassau Community College)

Yes, a lot of times people come to us and want to sell us courses, and textbook companies, but we don't buy them. (Coordinator, large, public, southern U.S. doctoral degree–granting institution)

However, some interviewees did reveal some partnerships involving content purchase and more extensive moves toward corporate connections. This was particularly the case for independent doctoral degree–granting institutions.

Canter first came to us in 1994 and that whole next year through 1995 the faculty had to adjust to the idea, as I said before, that you could have a quality program without students coming and sitting in a desk and listening to a lecture. There are other modes or models. So, there had to be a shifting of paradigms. It took about a year for that to happen. (Joy Edwards, Director of Graduate Studies, Texas Wesleyan University)

Clearly the relationships that have been longest in duration are [with] the for-profits, but we are not working with for-profits exclusively. (Program Manager, independent, western U.S. doctoral degree–granting institution)

It was a win-win situation. [The company] gave us resources we need for servers, ISBN, giving us the connections we needed for students. (Faculty and Program Director, HBCU)

The following specialized religious institution describes experimenting with a partnership agreement, an experience undoubtedly shared by many institutions.

We have experimented with that [partnerships with for-profit groups]. We have an experimental course with Jones Knowledge [Network]. But we have decided to predominantly use our own resources. (Jon Raibley, Assistant Director of Lifelong Learning Center, Western Seminary)

Notice in the following interview the process that is described of forming a partnership for needed technical competencies, and then discontinuing the agreement when less complex Internet technology came along.

Jones [Knowledge Network] became the sort of structure for all of this. Also they accessed the satellite time. Actually, our relationship with Jones was very good. What happened was that Jones after three years figured out that the Internet was the way it was going. They realized that the videotapes were going to be passé, and that everything was going to be on the Internet. Actually, what happens with the Internet could be done in-house. Why do we need to stay with Jones? Maybe we could do this ourselves. We have left Jones. We use Blackboard for our courses. (Warren Ashley, Director, Center for Mediated Instruction and Distance Learning, CSU Dominguez Hills)

The following passage shows that some of the leaders in distance learning have developed competencies and resources to the extent that they now themselves have services and educational products to sell.

Initially it was to make available our programs to companies. And as companies realize the importance of education in their business, they come to us with this need. We can fill that gap, and that's an accepted role for us. More recently we have worked with for-profit companies by actually becoming one of them. When we were looking for a software platform for all of our courses, there are a number of standard ones such as WebCT, Blackboard, Embanet, First Class. We didn't find one that had everything we needed, so we in fact created our own. In a couple of years programming came up with a program called [name of software] which has been just incredibly well accepted here. We literally have over a thousand courses now using [it], fully online courses, and to supplement regular campus courses. It was so successful that we decided, maybe we should sell this. So we created a for-profit company to market this across the country. I think fourteen institutions are using it now including Vanderbilt, and others are exploring it. So that's one way. The other is the international effort I mentioned. We joined with other universities to create what we call the Global University Alliance, a for-profit company, that will be delivering online programs worldwide. . . . We dropped the relationship with MEU [Mind Extension University]. That was part of the relationship with the commercial world. They wanted us to use their interface, and we couldn't justify that. The cable service that they were offering got us into five to seven million homes, but at this point we are broadcasting on a channel through PBS, and through the Web. Who knows how many homes we are getting into. . . . You look at NYU and they have a for-profit school, Maryland has a for-profit school, there's more and more. I think we are all trying to figure out how we can fit in this new world of e-learning. (Vice-President, large, independent, urban, eastern U.S. doctoral degree–granting institution)

For public institutions, partnerships often seem to take the form of collaborations with other nonprofit higher education institutions, or with other nonprofit organizations and government agencies.

We've talked to some public agencies about partnerships. The U.S. Attorney's Office in Minneapolis, with the Bureau of Criminal Investigation, with the Department of Natural Resources, and the City of St. Cloud to do some things. (John Burgeson, Dean of Continuing Education, St. Cloud State University)

Are you familiar with the California Virtual College? We are in Region Four, and through CVC4 we are getting these licenses. We're not paying out-of-pocket, and if I had to pay out-of-pocket we probably wouldn't be there yet. (Greg Chamberlain, Dean of Learning Resources, Bakersfield College)

The main one we are involved in is the NUDC, National University Degree Consortium. Currently, eleven universities, including Alabama, are involved in the consortium. All are traditional brick and mortar institutions like ourselves located all across the country. Primarily, the idea was to say you offer this, we offer that, let's market everything together. The organization has been around for over ten years and we are looking to add additional universities in the future. The idea behind NUDC is for universities with like interests to collaborate for marketing and information purposes. Our main marketing tool is our Web site. If a student visits our Web site, he/she will have the opportunity to choose from all of the distance programs available from the eleven member institutions. (Allan Guenther, Marketing Coordinator for Distance Education, the University of Alabama)

We do have a partnership with the community colleges, which I want to talk to you about. Another partnership we are working on right now is with the Internal Revenue Service, but the go-between is A. D. Little, a consulting company. They approached 16 institutions about developing online learning courses for the IRS. FSU is developing accounting courses. The agency reorganized and not everyone had the necessary training or education for the jobs that they were in. What the IRS is doing is working with universities to develop the courses they need. And when they [employees] complete the necessary courses, they can remain in their current positions or advance. If not, they drop back to where they were before. So it's developing into a competency-based, skill-building program nationwide for the IRS. Then we have an agreement with the Navy to offer some of our distance learning courses for Navy personnel worldwide. (Carole Hayes, Coordinator, External Relations and Development, Office for Distributed and Distance Learning, Florida State University)

The State itself has created Washington Online, the acronym is WAOL, and they're doing on a statewide level what we're doing. It involves most of the colleges in the state and it's mutating in an effort to be even more inclusive. There was a group of colleges in the beginning that didn't think WAOL was going about it in the most efficient way, so they started what was known as the Virtual Campus. Now those two things have merged and meshed because the Higher Education Coordinating Board didn't want to see two entities. We've now grown to the point that we now serve between six and seven thousand students. (Thornton Perry, Director of Distance Education, Bellevue Community College)

Some of the interviewees conveyed critical views of partnerships with for-profit organizations.

I think it is problematic when you have higher education institutions working with proprietary companies that are dedicated, and even bound by law, to care more about returning money [to investors] than . . . to caring about the quality of a product. If you can get away with making a low quality product and your investors are making a lot of money, you really have to go in that direction. You want to get both, but you can't. Now here that's not true. As a faculty member, I have no interest in making money. It's good that the institution is doing well, but that doesn't affect how I teach. So I'm going to work to deliver the best product, if you will. . . . When it comes to something like E-College, they're going to do the best they can to deliver a service to us, because they need us to buy their service. We get to be the determiners. I wouldn't want someone saying we had to use them, but it doesn't work that way, fortunately. . . . When it comes to an outside vendor and us-ing their services for, say, test taking, I worry about that a little more. Anything that, it isn't the right phrase but, is out of our locus of con-trol, our sphere of influence. And has motivations beyond what my motivation is for [using distance] learning, I'm suspect and want to seek control. (Don Cardinal, faculty member, Chapman University)

Others were more open to the possibility, particularly if the faculty make final academic decisions.

My first question to faculty is, how does that fit into your curriculum? I encourage the faculty to not reinvent the wheel. If a company has de-veloped good modules, why re-create them? I encourage faculty to look at these materials and use them if they meet the needs of the stu-dents for the first two years of college. I remind them to check what technical support, connectivity, management, and archiving is pro-vided by publishers on their servers. (Vivian Sinou, Dean, Distance and Mediated Learning, Foothill College)

ADMINISTRATIVE INNOVATIONS—COST SAVINGS (SEAT TIME/DYNAMIC SCHEDULING/LICENSED MATERIALS)

Distance learning was seen by some as leading to administrative innova-tions such as reduced seat time, flexible scheduling, and the use of prepared course materials which would bring cost savings to the institution. One comprehensive institution representative spoke about the reduction in class time leading to flexible scheduling:

So this is what I see happening, and by the way I see this happening for both distance learning and the campus courses, is that seat time is ir-relevant. It no longer exists; it doesn't matter how long or little you sit in the class in terms of how much you learn. So people will start to say for this particular class I need to meet four times for two hours. And that could be a campus class, or it could be a distance learning class. The only difference is that for the distance learning class you come here for those four meetings. There are other people who will say that I need to meet weekly, 14 times, Mondays. I taught a course called Effective College Teaching. What I said is, look, I looked over the objectives, we are going to do this asynchronous, but we need to meet once a week, Thursdays. What you should do is block off 120 minutes, but if we have accomplished our goals, we will only meet for about 30 minutes. But for another week, because we are talking about attitudes or values, we could be involved in a discussion for 120 minutes. It was interesting because it was a whole different way of looking at class meetings. . . . One of the interesting things that I think is going to happen is that institutions of higher education, if you have classes and they are not meeting twice a week, do you want to schedule that room every week? And if you don't, how do you make sure that you are going to have a room? And this is already being discussed: "dynamic scheduling." That may not be the way to schedule rooms. You might add a third more classes without adding any more bricks and mortar. (Warren Ashley, Director, Center for Mediated Instruction and Distance Learning, CSU Dominguez Hills)

The use of courses licensed from other organizations is one way institutions might reduce expenses. The survey found that 30.2% of the respondents purchased course content from other institutions (see Table 8.8). Community colleges are much more likely to lease courses from other organizations than are other types of institutions—42.0% compared to 22.9% and 27.8% for the other types (see Table 8.9). (Note: See previous note regarding variance in totals in crosstabulation calculations.) One interviewee pointed to the problem he sees in purchasing content from external sources.

Yes, when I was teaching I spent a year looking for the right Turbo Pascal textbook. It doesn't exist. I looked at probably 50 of them. The perfect course for any instructor probably doesn't exist when you buy it from someone else. . . . So I see [our] direction . . . is to do just that, buy the content of the course, and then the instructor, just like with a text,

Table 8.8
Use of Licensed Courses (Question 20)

Does your institution use whole courses licensed from other educational institutions?

		Frequency	Percent	Valid Percent	Cumulative Percent
Valid	yes	51	29.0	30.2	30.2
	no	118	67.0	69.8	100.0
	Total	169	96.0	100.0	
Missing	System	7	4.0		
Total		176	100.0		

Table 8.9
Use of Licensed Courses by Institution Type (Questions 2 & 20)

Highest degree your institution awards? * Does your institution use whole courses licensed from other educational institutions? Crosstabulation

			Does your institution use whole courses licensed from other educational institutions?		
			yes	no	Total
Highest degree your institution awards?	associate	Count	21	29	50
		% within Highest degree your institution awards?	42.0%	58.0%	100.0%
	bachelor's	Count	4	11	15
		% within Highest degree your institution awards?	26.7%	73.3%	100.0%
	master's	Count	11	37	48
		% within Highest degree your institution awards?	22.9%	77.1%	100.0%
	doctorate	Count	15	39	54
		% within Highest degree your institution awards?	27.8%	72.2%	100.0%
Total		Count	51	116	167
		% within Highest degree your institution awards?	30.5%	69.5%	100.0%

utilizes the content with the technology in the best way they see fit. We don't want to get into the business of providing the Big Mac hamburger that . . . you can buy anywhere else in the country. (Greg Chamberlain, Dean of Learning Resources, Bakersfield College)

BUDGET

Obviously, whether institutions are profiting economically from the use of distance learning is a key indicator in understanding if distance learning is commercializing higher education. First, and perhaps surprisingly, a substantial majority (72.2%) of the institutions have not even done a cost/benefit analysis of their programs (see Table 8.10). The survey results show that over two-thirds of the distance learning programs (68.3%) are at least partially fiscally subsidized (see Table 8.11). However, two-year institutions showed a much higher rate of subsidized activity at 93.4%, compared to 56.3% at master's degree–granting institutions and 61.1% at doctoral degree–granting institutions (see Table 8.12). (Note: Crosstabulation total variance as explained previously.) Asked in a different way, the respondents show a little rosier picture, with most (77.2%) either breaking even or making a profit (see Table 8.13). Although most institutions have not done a cost/benefit analysis, they still responded to more general ques-

Table 8.10
Cost/Benefit Analysis (Question 36)

Have you done a cost/benefit analysis of distance learning?

		Frequency	Percent	Valid Percent	Cumulative Percent
Valid	yes	47	26.7	27.8	27.8
	no	122	69.3	72.2	100.0
	Total	169	96.0	100.0	
Missing	System	7	4.0		
Total		176	100.0		

Table 8.11
Budget Subsidy (Question 16)

Is this administrative unit budgetarily described as

		Frequency	Percent	Valid Percent	Cumulative Percent
Valid	subsidized	67	38.1	40.9	40.9
	partial subsidized	45	25.6	27.4	68.3
	self-supporting	52	29.5	31.7	100.0
	Total	164	93.2	100.0	
Missing	System	12	6.8		
Total		176	100.0		

Table 8.12
Budget Subsidy by Institution Type (Questions 2 & 16)

Highest degree your institution awards? * Is this administrative unit budgetarily described as Crosstabulation

			subsidized	partial subsidized	self-supporting	Total
Highest degree your institution awards?	associate	Count	30	12	3	45
		% within Highest degree your institution awards?	66.7%	26.7%	6.7%	100.0%
	bachelor's	Count	5	4	6	15
		% within Highest degree your institution awards?	33.3%	26.7%	40.0%	100.0%
	master's	Count	15	12	21	48
		% within Highest degree your institution awards?	31.3%	25.0%	43.8%	100.0%
	doctorate	Count	17	16	21	54
		% within Highest degree your institution awards?	31.5%	29.6%	38.9%	100.0%
Total		Count	67	44	51	162
		% within Highest degree your institution awards?	41.4%	27.2%	31.5%	100.0%

Table 8.13
Economic Status (Question 18)

Which of the following best describes the current economic status of your distance learning program

		Frequency	Percent	Valid Percent	Cumulative Percent
Valid	large deficit	8	4.5	4.9	4.9
	deficit	29	16.5	17.9	22.8
	break even	73	41.5	45.1	67.9
	profit	48	27.3	29.6	97.5
	large profit	4	2.3	2.5	100.0
	Total	162	92.0	100.0	
Missing	System	14	8.0		
Total		176	100.0		

tions about economic status. As most of the respondents have administrative responsibility for distance learning programs at their own institution, it is possible that these budgetary data are somewhat slanted toward the appearance of profitability. Furthermore, part of the reason for this apparent discrepancy has to do with the complex budget at public institutions, where the notion of "profit" is problematic. When broken out by institutional type we find that doctoral degree–granting (36.4% combined) and master's degree–granting (39.6% combined) institutions report either a "profit" or "large profit" more often than two-year institutions (21.4% combined) (see Table 8.14).

Another indicator of academic capitalism is the use of outside vendors for marketing purposes. Most (76.3%) of those surveyed do not use such services (see Table 8.15). When broken down by institutional type we find that there was little difference in the responses (see Table 8.16).

Furthermore, we saw from the research literature review in Chapter 4 that some institutions view distance learning as an administrative innovation, one that allows them to serve more students for less money. In contrast to this point of view, many surveyed in the current study do not see distance learning as an innovation in this way, and therefore perhaps not as a way to increase revenue. When asked whether they view distance learning in higher education as an administrative innovation, only 26.2% responded "yes"; 33.9% answered "maybe," and 39.9% "no" (see Table 8.17). When analyzed by institutional type we find that there is little difference, although doctoral degree–granting institutions responded "no" at a higher rate (49.1%) than either two-year institutions (38.8%) or master's degree-granting institutions (32.7%) (see Table 8.18).

Table 8.14
Economic Status by Institutional Type (Questions 2 & 18)

Highest degree your institution awards? * Which of the following best describes the current economic status of your distance learning program? Crosstabulation

			Which of the following best describes the current economic status of your distance learning program					Total
			large deficit	deficit	break even	profit	large profit	
Highest degree your institution awards?	associate	Count		11	22	9		42
		% within Highest degree your institution awards?		26.2%	52.4%	21.4%		100.0%
	bachelor's	Count	2	2	8	3		15
		% within Highest degree your institution awards?	13.3%	13.3%	53.3%	20.0%		100.0%
	master's	Count	4	6	19	18	1	48
		% within Highest degree your institution awards?	8.3%	12.5%	39.6%	37.5%	2.1%	100.0%
	doctorate	Count	2	9	24	17	3	55
		% within Highest degree your institution awards?	3.6%	16.4%	43.6%	30.9%	5.5%	100.0%
Total		Count	8	28	73	47	4	160
		% within Highest degree your institution awards?	5.0%	17.5%	45.6%	29.4%	2.5%	100.0%

Table 8.15
Marketing Service Use (Question 21)

Are you using any kind of course brokering service to market distance learning courses to non-matriculated students?

		Frequency	Percent	Valid Percent	Cumulative Percent
Valid	yes	40	22.7	23.7	23.7
	no	129	73.3	76.3	100.0
	Total	169	96.0	100.0	
Missing	System	7	4.0		
Total		176	100.0		

EFFECT OF REVENUE INSTITUTIONAL MOTIVE ON ADMINISTRATIVE PRACTICES

When correlating those respondents who indicate that pursuing new sources of revenue is a motivation for using distance learning with other key administrative practices such as utilizing licensed courses, brokers, stipends for course development, teams for course development, proctored tests, and adjunct faculty to teach courses, the following was found. Among the 68 institutions that reported they were seeking revenue, they were more likely than the total average of the respondents to use brokers for marketing (36.8% versus 23.7%). This revenue-seeking group was also more likely than the total average of the respondents to compensate faculty with a stipend (19.1% versus 14.0%) (see Table 8.19). There was little difference between revenue-seeking institutions and the total average in the use of whole courses licensed from other institutions (29.4% versus 30.2%).

Table 8.16
Marketing Service Use by Institutional Type (Questions 2 & 21)

Highest degree your institution awards? * Are you using any kind of course brokering service to market distance learning courses to non-matriculated students? Crosstabulation

			Are you using any kind of course brokering service to market distance learning courses to non-matriculated students?		Total
			yes	no	
Highest degree your institution awards?	associate	Count	12	38	50
		% within Highest degree your institution awards?	24.0%	76.0%	100.0%
	bachelor's	Count	4	11	15
		% within Highest degree your institution awards?	26.7%	73.3%	100.0%
	master's	Count	10	37	47
		% within Highest degree your institution awards?	21.3%	78.7%	100.0%
	doctorate	Count	13	42	55
		% within Highest degree your institution awards?	23.6%	76.4%	100.0%
Total		Count	39	128	167
		% within Highest degree your institution awards?	23.4%	76.6%	100.0%

Table 8.17
Administrative Innovation (Question 23)

Do you view distance learning in higher education as an administrative innovation?

		Frequency	Percent	Valid Percent	Cumulative Percent
Valid	yes	44	25.0	26.2	26.2
	maybe	57	32.4	33.9	60.1
	no	67	38.1	39.9	100.0
	Total	168	95.5	100.0	
Missing	System	8	4.5		
Total		176	100.0		

Undoubtedly, this is a result of the community colleges' tendency to use licensed courses heavily.

The use of adjunct faculty was, surprisingly, not significantly different for revenue-seeking institutions (75.4% versus 76.6% 0–25% range) (see Table 8.20). In terms of course development, consistent with the University of Phoenix and British Open University models, it was found that those institutions indicating a revenue motive use teams slightly more than

Table 8.18
Administrative Innovation by Institutional Type (Questions 2 & 23)

Highest degree your institution awards? * Do you view distance learning in higher education as an administrative innovation? Crosstabulation

			Do you view distance learning in higher education as an administrative innovation?			
			yes	maybe	no	Total
Highest degree your institution awards?	associate	Count	11	19	19	49
		% within Highest degree your institution awards?	22.4%	38.8%	38.8%	100.0%
	bachelor's	Count	6	4	5	15
		% within Highest degree your institution awards?	40.0%	26.7%	33.3%	100.0%
	master's	Count	13	20	16	49
		% within Highest degree your institution awards?	26.5%	40.8%	32.7%	100.0%
	doctorate	Count	14	13	26	53
		% within Highest degree your institution awards?	26.4%	24.5%	49.1%	100.0%
Total		Count	44	56	66	166
		% within Highest degree your institution awards?	26.5%	33.7%	39.8%	100.0%

the average (10% versus 7.6%) (see Table 8.21). In terms of academic oversight issues, those indicating a revenue motive use proctored tests less frequently than the overall institutional average (15.9% versus 22.8% "always") (see Table 8.22).

Interviewees did talk about the economics of distance learning with various emphasis depending on the public or independent status of their institutions. The following independent institution emphasized the disadvantage of private universities in pricing.

> Yeah, distance learning costs a lot of money. And we can't really afford to distribute it for three or four or five students. The big difference is that it has to be responsive to student needs. . . . The other disadvantage is that we're a private school, and we have to charge more than the University of Nebraska or California State is doing. My whole work history before this was in state institutions, and I remember how much we hated to raise tuition. Then, I came here, and we have to charge five times as much . . . how can we compete? We have to do something special. (Vice-President, large, independent, urban, eastern U.S. doctoral degree–granting institution)

A representative from a large public institution emphasized that new revenue generated from distance learning is reinvested in the department.

> Money generated is put back into [distance learning programs] to grow it over the next few years. (Carole Hayes, Coordinator, External Rela-

Table 8.19
Revenue-Seeking Motivation & Payment of Stipend (Questions 6 & 24)

New source of revenue * How are full-time faculty compensated for teaching distance learning format courses? Crosstabulation

		How are full-time faculty compensated for teaching distance learning format courses?									Total
		regular load with normal enrollment limits	regular load with no ceiling on enrollment	regular load with additional pay after seat maximum	with additional preparation time	on overload basis	additional stipend	regular load for in-person class, per head for remote student	other	do not use full-time faculty	
New source of revenue yes	Count	21	5	4	6	6	13	2	8	3	68
	% within New source of revenue	30.9%	7.4%	5.9%	8.8%	8.8%	19.1%	2.9%	11.8%	4.4%	100.0%
Total	Count	21	5	4	6	6	13	2	8	3	68
	% within New source of revenue	30.9%	7.4%	5.9%	8.8%	8.8%	19.1%	2.9%	11.8%	4.4%	100.0%

Table 8.20
Revenue-Seeking Motivation & Use of Adjunct Faculty (Questions 6 & 31)

New source of revenue * What is the percentage of faculty teaching distance learning courses that are classified as adjunct faculty? Crosstabulation

			What is the percentage of faculty teaching distance learning courses that are classified as adjunct faculty?				Total
			0-25	26-50	51-75	76+	
New source of revenue	yes	Count	52	8	4	5	69
		% within New source of revenue	75.4%	11.6%	5.8%	7.2%	100.0%
Total		Count	52	8	4	5	69
		% within New source of revenue	75.4%	11.6%	5.8%	7.2%	100.0%

tions and Development, Office for Distributed and Distance Learning, Florida State University)

According to the following community college, the distance learning budget is self-supporting to some degree.

> In fact throughout my experience, distance education was self-funded. We had to drum up enough students for these courses. The faculty teaching the courses were moonlighting, a fourth course with the three that they normally taught. We've been kind of like a small business. As time has gone on we've been incorporated in the larger campus fiscal apparatus. . . . We have been included in the institutional fiscal accounting, but there are portions that are self-funded. (Thornton Perry, Director of Distance Education, Bellevue Community College)

CHANGE

One interviewee who reflected on the change process at his institution pointed out that leadership support and a flat hierarchy enabled the implementation of distance learning.

> There's very little hierarchy to the administration. There's also a sense that if you don't screw up, there is a lot of freedom. And we were lucky we didn't have a screwup. I was allowed to go out and investigate things, and my staff did the same things. So we had a high-energy group with enough resources to do things. So we worked with faculty and went out and did things. There was no master plan, and . . . because of the changes in technology it would be hard to have a plan. (Warren Ashley, Director, Center for Mediated Instruction and Distance Learning, CSU Dominguez Hills)

In the following interview, note how technology seems to push change along.

> I think the leadership here and the administration recognize that there are some changes that have to take place. And none of us know if we are doing the right thing or the wrong thing. But sitting still is almost certainly the wrong thing. So we're trying a number of things and watching them closely. Technology was the catalyst to make all of these things possible. . . . It's hard to change institutions; they don't change rapidly. (Vice-President, large, independent, urban, eastern U.S. doctoral degree–granting institution)

One institution expressed concern about distance learning change occurring too rapidly.

Table 8.21
Revenue-Seeking Motivation & Team Course Development (Questions 6 & 34)

New source of revenue * Are courses typically developed by faculty/instructors through Crosstabulation

| | | | Are courses typically developed by faculty/instructors through | | | Total |
			teams	individuals	both	
New source of revenue	yes	Count	7	38	25	70
		% within New source of revenue	10.0%	54.3%	35.7%	100.0%
Total		Count	7	38	25	70
		% within New source of revenue	10.0%	54.3%	35.7%	100.0%

Table 8.22
Revenue-Seeking Motivation & Proctored Tests (Questions 6 & 35)

New source of revenue * Do you generally require a proctored test for course completion? Crosstabulation

| | | | Do you generally require a proctored test for course completion? | | | Total |
			always	sometimes	never	
New source of revenue	yes	Count	11	51	7	69
		% within New source of revenue	15.9%	73.9%	10.1%	100.0%
Total		Count	11	51	7	69
		% within New source of revenue	15.9%	73.9%	10.1%	100.0%

I'm excited about it. I love it when people stir the pot. Obviously, sometimes stirring the pot can go too far—it depends on who gets to make that judgment. I like it when you can stir the pot, and there is time to resolve the issues as they come up. When I don't like it is when too many issues are coming up and there isn't time to resolve them, and to come up with new ideas. (Don Cardinal, faculty member, Chapman University)

CHANGING FACULTY ROLE

Besides the changes in compensation, many of the interviewees spoke about changes in faculty role and duties.

I like this discussion about changing roles. See, that's something we should always have been talking about before. We've been doing this [education] for two hundred years and we've never talked about it. It only came up when we had the book. See, [the Dean] has the view that when you use your own book in a class you teach, that the money you make should be returned back into the School of Education. I understand the point, and most people here agree. That's the way we operate here. We felt that was morally right. Now apply that to the online environment. Say I teach a course for the School of Education. What if someone comes to me and asks me to teach a version of that over here? They want to pay me an extra fee—overload. Is that okay too? So, it opens up a lot of areas that I find fascinating. The questions aren't just about online education. They relate to all we have been doing before. (Don Cardinal, faculty member, Chapman University)

One interviewee described the power faculty still currently have over participation in distance learning.

But by and large from where we sit the faculty have a lot of discretion. And so if a faculty member wasn't interested, they wouldn't participate. We don't broadcast all courses; they are selected in conjunction with the departments. (Vice-President, large, independent, urban, eastern U.S. doctoral degree–granting institution)

One respondent described how distance learning is changing the requirement of physical presence on campus, and even leading to salary adjustments because of nonparticipation in institutional governance.

It's touching on a whole new thing. We have faculty teaching their entire load at a distance. The Web-authoring person is in Albuquerque, the anthropologist is somewhere down in California, the economics person teaches from his condominium in Puget Sound. In some cases there are salary adjustments because of their nonparticipation in governance. Other faculty are wanting to create hybrid courses that only meet a couple of times a term. A couple of them went out on their own and collaborated with a publishing company to put their courses on Web sites that are not our own. The issue is under study as I speak to you. The institution has some concerns because you have no control over what kind of content is going in, and more importantly, what level of interactivity there is. It hasn't happened until this very quarter. A couple of faculty members were bit by the bug, or didn't want to deal with the commute, I don't know. (Thornton Perry, Director of Distance Education, Bellevue Community College)

A representative from a specialized religious institution related how faculty resistance to distance learning was overcome by a focus on quality.

Historically, there was resistance to distance education. It was seen as a threat to job security. That is not so much a problem now. We work with the faculty and are concerned that what we do is high quality, and that it is equivalent in terms of content and academic integrity to what they would do in class. (Jon Raibley, Assistant Director of Lifelong Learning Center, Western Seminary)

Some interviewees spoke about how distance learning is leading to positive changes in faculty teaching approaches.

It encourages faculty to stay current. The environment lends itself to renewal and change. (Vivian Sinou, Dean, Distance and Mediated Learning, Foothill College)

Since I've started to teach online I've increased my physical office hours from six hours a week to nine hours a week. It's been about two years now. And it's better. These are hours I actually give to the secretary, I don't have control over them. This is in addition to other times when students drop by. So what happened is that I saw what was happening in the online course with students really increasing learning from online office hours. So I asked myself, if I'm getting better learning online because I'm with them longer, won't I also get better learning if I'm with them longer in the traditional class during office hours? What about those students that aren't online, shouldn't they get my extra time also? If putting in more time outside the classroom produces better learning, was it because of the email, or was it just the extra time? (Don Cardinal, faculty member, Chapman University)

One can see from the results presented in this chapter that administrative practices vary greatly in the way distance learning is organized in American higher education. Nevertheless, indication of the commercialization of higher education through distance learning is seen in the lack of stipends paid to faculty for course development, the high percentage of respondents claiming institutional ownership of course materials, corporate management approaches, corporate partnerships, and claims of profitability. In contrast, use of part-time faculty was surprisingly low, and there appears to be little difference in administrative practices, including payment of stipends, use of adjunct faculty, team course development, and proctored tests for those institutions with revenue-seeking motivations. In the final chapter I will draw some conclusions about these data, particularly as they relate to the research questions connecting specific practices to institutional motive. In the next chapter, I turn to the data on pedagogical methods and their correlation to institutional profit motives.

CHAPTER

Administrative Motive
Effect on Pedagogy

In this chapter the hypothesis that a revenue institutional motive might adversely affect pedagogical practice in distance learning courses is tested. In the following series of tables, the responses of those institutions reporting explicit focus on access are compared with those explicitly seeking new sources of revenue. For those indicating access as a primary reason for using distance learning, the survey respondents saw the importance of attention to converting traditional course material to distance learning formats. Those indicating a revenue motive were slightly less in agreement with this pedagogical focus (62.9% compared to 63.7% "strongly agree) (see Table 9.1). Those pursuing revenue had a slightly lower focus on interaction (38.6% compared to 44.7% "strongly agree") (see Table 9.2).

Collaboration as a pedagogical approach was of slightly less interest to those seeking additional revenue (25.7% compared to 32.3% "strongly agree") (see Table 9.3).

Simulations were also less common for this revenue-seeking group (17.9% compared to 21.2% "strongly agree) (see Table 9.4). Those seeking additional revenue also responded at a lower rate of agreement to a concern for computer interface navigation issues (37.7% compared to 39.9% "strongly agree") (see Table 9.5).

Table 9.1
Access/Revenue Motivation & Converting Course Material (Questions 6 & 40)

Questions about how best to convert course material to distance learning format are of great importance-- crosstabulation

	strongly agree	agree	disagree	strongly disagree
Access	63.7%	31.2%	3.8%	1.3%
Revenue	62.9%	31.4%	4.3%	1.4%

Table 9.2
Access/Revenue Motivation & Interaction (Questions 6 & 41)

Courses include significant interaction with other students--crosstabulation

	strongly agree	agree	disagree	strongly disagree
Access	44.7%	41.5%	12.6%	1.3%
Revenue	38.6%	47.1%	4.3%	1.4%

Table 9.3
Access/Revenue Motivation & Collaboration (Questions 6 & 42)

Courses offer opportunity to collaborate with other students on projects--crosstabulation

	strongly agree	agree	disagree	strongly disagree
Access	32.3%	53.2%	12.7%	1.9%
Revenue	25.7%	58.6%	14.3%	1.4%

Table 9.4
Access/Revenue Motivation & Simulations (Questions 6 & 43)

Courses include simulations and/or case studies--crosstabulation

	strongly agree	agree	disagree	strongly disagree
Access	21.2%	67.3%	10.3%	1.3%
Revenue	17.9%	70.1%	11.9%	0%

Table 9.5
Access/Revenue Motivation & Navigation (Questions 6 & 44)

Great care is taken in understanding how students navigate through the course software--crosstabulation

	strongly agree	agree	disagree	strongly disagree
Access	39.9%	44.9%	11.4%	3.8 %
Revenue	37.7%	42.0%	17.4%	2.9%

A focus on a tutorial model with one-on-one interaction was more common in the group of those motivated by access rather than revenue (26.1% compared to 21.4% "strongly agree") (see Table 9.6).

The course development process tends to be shorter for those explicitly motivated by revenue (70.6% compared to 61.8% develop courses in less than six months) (see Table 9.7).

Those institutions with a stated goal of pursuing new revenue sources indicate a lower response to developing courses specifically for distance learning (18.8% versus 27.4%) (see Table 9.8).

No significant difference was reported in assessment of distance learning courses between those with access and revenue motivations (87.1% for those with revenue motivation compared to 86.2% for those with an access motivation responding "yes") (see Table 9.9).

From these comparisons, one can see that overall there was a slightly higher and broader sophistication in pedagogical approaches for those indicating access rather than pursuit of new sources of revenue as an institutional motivation. The largest variance in self-reported concern for pedagogical issues came in interaction (6.1% difference in "strongly agree" responses), collaboration with other students (6.6% difference in "strongly agree" responses), and tutorial methods (4.8% difference in "strongly agree" responses). While these differences are not statistically significant, they are troubling. Two questions focusing on the course development process revealed a greater discrepancy between institutions with access motivations versus those with revenue motivations for using distance learning. Those with a revenue motivation were more likely than those with an access motivation to develop courses in less than six months (70.6% compared to 61.8%). While one might argue that developing courses in less time may be a function of greater efficiency, not lower quality, the question centering on how often course material is developed specifically for the distance learning courses points directly to quality standards and pedagogical sophistication. In response to the question of which most closely reflects the course development process, those institutions with an access motiva-

Table 9.6
Access/Revenue Motivation & Tutoring (Questions 6 & 45)

Courses are like one-on-one tutoring with the faculty member, providing rich and prompt feedback to the students--crosstabulation

	strongly agree	agree	disagree	strongly disagree
Access	26.1%	47.1%	22.3%	4.5%
Revenue	21.4%	47.1%	22.9%	8.6%

Table 9.7
Access/Revenue Motivation & Development Length (Questions 6 & 47)

How long does it generally take to develop a new distance learning format course?--crosstabulation

	<6 months	1 year	2 years
Access	61.8%	36.3%	1.9%
Revenue	70.6%	27.9%	1.5%

Table 9.8
Access/Revenue Motivation & Development Process (Questions 6 & 48)

Which of the following most closely reflects the course development process?--crosstabulation

	existing course material automated by technology	existing course material automated, with some new material	all course material developed specifically for DL courses
Access	15.3%	57.3%	27.4%
Revenue	15.9%	65.2%	18.8%

Table 9.9
Access/Revenue Motivation & Tutoring (Questions 6 & 45)

Is assessment of student learning similar or the same as in traditional courses?--crosstabulation

	yes	no
Access	86.2%	13.8%
Revenue	87.1%	12.9%

tion were more likely to develop all course materials specifically for the distance learning courses by a margin of 8.6% (27.4% compared to 18.8%).

In the next chapter I draw conclusions from the results presented in this and the previous chapters. Additionally, I evaluate the results in relationship to the questions posed at the start of this study. Finally, I make some broad observations about what has been learned from this study of distance learning in American higher education.

CHAPTER 10

Conclusion

One who attempts to generalize about American higher education is going down a very treacherous path. This complexity was found again and again in the study, particularly in the interviews, where the diversity of motivation for using distance learning was striking. Regional comprehensives were often concerned with access in geographical areas. Religious-based colleges spoke about seeking ways to spread their religious doctrine around the world and to serve practicing members of their ministry. Specialized institutions recognized a need to attract students from wide geographical areas. HBCUs and community colleges focused on access issues. Research institutions sought ways to cement relationships with industry. Overall, the data indicate to me that universities are generally implementing distance learning by sticking very closely to traditional administrative and pedagogical methods, and, most important, using regular faculty. In my mind this has assured both a baseline level of quality and mediocrity. This chapter summarizes the main points of the research literature reviews and then analyzes the data within a broader context. Conclusions are drawn regarding the original research questions, subquestions, and implicit hypotheses. Finally, implications of the conclusions are considered, recommendations for administrative practices are made, and an agenda for future research in the field is outlined.

A review of previous studies of distance learning in higher education was followed by the discussion of its historical development from its origins in the Chautauqua Movement and at the University of Chicago, through the use of instructional television and Internet-based courses. Additionally, relevant literature on educational change theory as it relates to technology, the role of the faculty, leading models of distance learning, and evolving best practices was reviewed. The data gathered for study and reported in Chapter 6 indicated how institutional motivation to use distance learning affects specific administrative practices by looking at such issues as course approval process, where courses are administratively housed, faculty compensation practices, partnership agreements, marketing practices, and assessment. A review of distance learning's history in America reveals that this format was not used to replace traditional higher education, but instead was aimed consistently at nontraditional student populations lacking access. Distance learning courses grew out of the University Extension Movement, beginning at the University of Chicago and then spreading widely throughout higher education. Particularly with correspondence courses, a history of serving different populations in more flexible ways sometimes led to poor quality and confused pedagogical approaches. The literature shows that innovation and change in higher education are often difficult, and that faculty play a key role. An examination of recent literature on distance learning administration reveals that prominent models focus on altering traditional higher education organizational structures. Finally, recent attempts to construct best practices standards for distance learning rely heavily on traditional measures of academic quality.

The third chapter turned toward the current state of research on the pedagogy of distance learning. In examining the implications of different institutional motives for the use of distance learning, the resulting effect on teaching/learning is of primary concern. In order to judge the sophistication of an institutional approach to distance learning pedagogy, a general understanding of research in this field was needed. Indicators of how institutional motivation to adopt distance learning are affecting pedagogical approaches were seen in the studies on course development and the prevalence of sophisticated pedagogical approaches, including collaboration, simulations, and the attention to interaction issues, computer interface design, and navigational strategies.

Chapter 4 focused on market approaches to university administration in order to help clarify the way this trend might play a part in the motivation to use distance learning. Evidence of market model approaches to distance learning is apparent in data revealing attempts to reduce labor expenses through technology, in copyright practices that give universities an accumulation of fixed intellectual capital, and through administrative approaches involving collaborations with businesses. When looking at current trends toward market models in higher education, it was useful to analyze proprietary and vocational school education for similarities to and differences from traditional higher education, characteristics of the schools and their students, curriculum, and staffing. Finally, because this topic has become the center of a heated debate about the commercialization of the academy, the growing literature on the subject of collaborations between business and higher education was reviewed.

One can see from the data presented in Chapter 6 that the explicit reason for using distance learning primarily is access. The hypothesis that distance learning format courses are implemented in higher education to increase revenue was disproved by this simple direct questioning. The second most common response was a belief in the pedagogical advantages of distance learning. Figure 10.1 shows the survey's results regarding explicit reasons for using distance learning.

The first impression received from the data returned in this study is that institutional motive for using distance learning is a combination of providing access and increasing learning through new teaching methods. However, is this the whole story?

Although the study included a rich diversity of institutional types, a pattern was discovered in comparing two-year to doctoral degree–granting institutions. This study shows that community colleges have different attitudes toward distance learning than doctoral degree–granting institutions. Two-year institutions played more of a leading role in the development of distance learning in America than four-year institutions. An administrator from a state university commented on the leading role the community colleges have played.

Figure 10.1
Reasons for Using DL (Question 6)

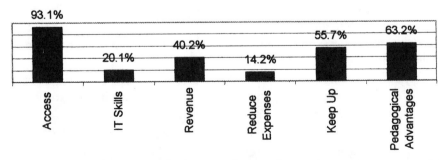

Note: Respondents could give multiple reasons for using distance learning in response to this question.

> The community colleges have traditionally been in the forefront with this because of their desire and mandate to meet community needs. . . . For instance, in Florida the community colleges were established by statute in the 1950s with the requirement that there must be access to a college within 50 miles of any citizen. In a way that is the original distance learning in Florida, if you take the colleges out to the people where they are. (Carole Hayes, Coordinator, External Relations and Development, Office for Distributed and Distance Learning, Florida State University)

Although individual four-year institutions have also been distance learning leaders, they have not been as active as a group until recently. In addition to an obvious focus on access, two-year institutions are more likely to see providing information technology skills as important, which fits clearly with their vocational education emphasis. While two-year institutions have in many ways been leaders in distance education in the past, research institutions are now apparently leading in developing distance learning programs with explicit revenue motivations, aimed in many instances at the corporate market. This point is emphasized by the fact that doctoral degree–granting institutions, at a rate higher than other types of institutions, indicated that pursuing new sources of revenue was a motivation (see Figure 10.2).

Therefore, if one is looking for evidence of academic capitalism, the focus immediately shifts to the doctoral degree–granting institutions because they are explicitly using distance learning both to develop new revenue sources and to encourage ties with industry. In addition to the survey data, we saw in Chapter 6 that the interviews supported this analysis that research institutions are concentrating on using distance learning to forge corporate relationships. Although community colleges have concerns about the economics of distance learning, they appear predominantly driven by their mission to provide access.

Figure 10.2
Revenue Seeking and Institutional Type (Questions 2 & 6) (Highest degree your institution awards?)

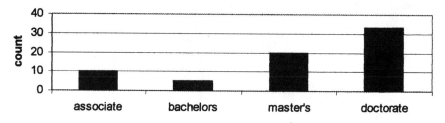

The hypothesis that distance learning format courses are implemented in higher education primarily in order to increase revenue was disproved. However, it is clear that the pursuit of revenue is one of the factors that go into the decision-making process, particularly for doctoral degree–granting institutions. Additionally, one must consider the source of these data. As in most cases the respondents represent the institution in relationship to distance learning efforts, it is likely that they want to put their efforts in the best light possible. We saw in Table 6.15 that, when asked if pursuing new revenue was an overall institutional concern, the majority in all classifications responded "yes" or "maybe" (56.4% "yes" for doctoral degree–granting institutions). One needs to separate the rhetoric from the reality here in evaluating the data. Furthermore, in one sense access could be viewed as seeking enrollments, or the pursuit of revenue. For many institutions, seeking increased enrollments is a clear motivation removed from the distance learning question. On the other hand, in the interviews it was clear that many of the subjects (especially the community college and HBCU representatives) were strongly motivated by wanting to include new nontraditional populations in their institutions.

Finally, it is important to distinguish between the hypothesis here addressed about explicitly seeking new revenue sources and the general connection with academic capitalism. While strictly speaking the hypothesis was disproved by direct questioning, the more general connection of distance learning to the commercialization of higher education is strongly indicated.

The issue of who initiated distance learning at an institution tells us about motive and how that relates to administrative structure. Figure 10.3 shows that top administrators and continuing education administrators were more than twice as likely to lead the implementation push for dis-

Figure 10.3
Who Initiated Distance Learning (Questions 13) (Who initiated the use of distance learning courses at your institution?)

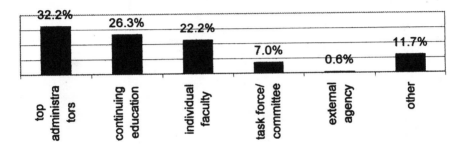

tance learning than individual faculty. Although we saw from institutional histories that faculty members sometimes initiated distance learning through an interest in technology, or a belief in the pedagogical advantages, overall this movement appears to be driven mainly by administrators.

The review of the history of distance learning in America revealed that it was aimed at the adult education market, not at the traditional undergraduate population. It is important for this study to consider whether distance learning courses are developed through university extension units or through traditional academic departments to understand who is in control and the intended audience. When asked where distance learning was administratively housed, respondents indicated that continuing education was the most common location (see Figure 10.4).

While certainly we learned from the interviews and the survey that these programs have normal academic oversight, the fact that they are so often located outside academic departments indicates to a large degree how they are regarded internally. As many continuing education departments are either self-supporting in public environments or typically seen as revenue generators in independent environments, one can argue that if distance learning is located in these externally aimed departments, they are viewed as revenue-generating programs. Although we saw from the interviews that many distance learning programs, particularly at four-year institutions, are rooted in academic departments, generally this is a continuing education activity.

If we look at how the motivation of seeking new sources of revenue affects administrative practices, we find that those institutions motivated by a pursuit of new sources of revenue used course brokers and compensated faculty with stipends at slightly higher response rates (see Figure 10.5). Course brokers are used to help "sell" courses to other institutions and indi-

Figure 10.4
Where Administratively Housed (Question 15)

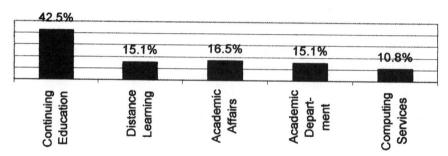

Figure 10.5
Administrative Comparison (Questions 6, 20, 21, 24, 31)

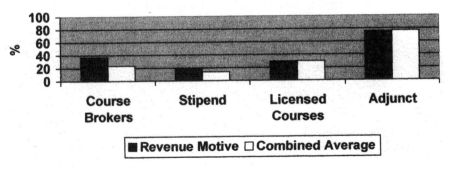

viduals and are obviously a revenue-seeking activity. The reasons these institutions pay stipends might be more varied. However, one likely result is that stipends imply a work-for-hire arrangement and can lead to an assumption of institutional ownership (although one should note here that community colleges have claimed institutional ownership more than any other institutional type). Those seeking new revenue through distance learning tend to use licensed courses slightly less, and this is undoubtedly a result of two-year institutions' widespread use of such resources. Finally, revenue-seeking institutions reported using adjunct faculty a little less. This last issue is interesting, because it illustrates how revenue-seeking distance learning attempts typically have begun in the heart of the university, with at least initial regular faculty involvement.

Some respondents commented directly on the problem of administrative structure and location of distance learning within the institution. They particularly focused on what happens when distance learning is located within a continuing education unit in terms of its function within the institution, and how it is regarded internally. As one interviewee from a specialized religious institution observed:

> In my twelve years we've bounced back and forth from being considered an academic program and being considered a service provider. I'm not sure myself where we currently are. Our strategy is that we are academic rather than service, that we are part of the development effort to expand the number of students. (Jon Raibley, Assistant Director of Lifelong Learning Center, Western Seminary)

One respondent commented directly on the for-profit nature of continuing education and what happens when it is connected to distance learning.

If I was in charge, would I lobby to have the unit removed from the College of Lifelong Learning, as it is now conceived, because of the [negative] baggage that comes with the poor reputation that the Academic Centers have had in the past? Once that reputation is created, it is tough to change. Then you throw in the online courses, the role of Extended Education has complicated the matter greatly. It's [Extended Education Department] an ideal place to put the online courses, particularly when you find that certain [academic] departments are ill-equipped or unwilling to put their core curriculum in this format—what an ideal mix that is. . . . So the cash cow notion and continuing education is there. And I think we are still there today. I don't think any university has continuing education for purely academic reasons. And I don't think anyone in California can say that. This is the role of the community colleges; the state has said we are going to spend money to educate anyone who wants to be educated for very low cost. It's very competitive, and you are fighting a free source of education. The state has said that the community colleges are to do this. Where does continuing education fit in for a private university? What benefit does it have for a private university? If there were a cost for it [continuing education], which is the acid test, would the institution keep it? I'd say that answer to that question is no, and it would be no for all independent institutions. (Don Cardinal, faculty member, Chapman University)

One institution illustrated the way that distance learning is causing them to reconfigure their administrative structure.

That [administrative structure of distance learning] is changing here also. The media production group since I've been here has been charged with generating funds. That means that we did everything that the university charged us with doing, but if we had some capacity beyond that we went out and marketed that to the local community. And that generated funds which allowed us to buy new equipment and stay up to the state of the art. So that has made us respond to community needs, create shorter, modular programs, pursue grants, but ultimately it means you have to be responsive and react rather rapidly. An example might be teaching a Java program, but the industry around you needs a Java plus program, or a Java script program. The academic program simply isn't at that level now. So we need to have a program that meets current needs. That's hard to do in a traditional academic program because it needs to go through committees and reviews and all sorts of analysis, and by the time it is approved we need the next generation of it. So that's been a problem, as well as an advantage. It helps us keep current. My office has always reported to the Academic Vice President's office. In the past there was discussion of moving us into Information Systems, but I think it was wise to keep us in the academic side of the house because the technology affects them so much. Now we're at a point where a lot of the real growth is in the distance students. We'll continue to have the brick and mortar campus, but we will expand the number of distance students. So we're setting up branch campuses, we're expanding distance learning, we're setting up custom programs in cooperation with corporations and government agencies. We've found it difficult to do all of this in the current configuration. So we've gotten approval for a new school here. . . . That school, which will be able to offer degrees, and has oversight by the academic side of the university, will have its own faculty, but the faculty will not have tenure. So, it will operate a little bit differently. (Vice-President, large, independent, urban, eastern U.S. doctoral degree–granting institution)

This last institution is clearly changing its administrative structure radically to accommodate the needs of external students through distance learning, and this change includes a discarding of tenure.

FACULTY—THE KEY FACTOR IN THE STUDY

In many ways, in answering the questions posed at the beginning of the study, the data on faculty are central to an understanding of institutional motives as they are played out in practice. In Chapter 4, a brief sketch of the economics of distance learning revealed the crucial role a repositioned faculty has in making distance learning work on a budgetary level. The survey results show that the majority are paid as regular load with normal enrollment limits (37.3%). Agreements for compensation as regular load with no ceiling on enrollment (6.0%) and regular load with additional pay after seat maximum (3.6%), when combined with the previous general regular load figure, total almost half of the responses (46.9%). On the key question of payment of a stipend for teaching distance learning courses, only 14.5% reported such a practice. The granting of additional preparation time (9.0%) and payment on an overload basis (9.6%) were less commonly reported by respondents. Only 4.2% of the respondents report not using full-time faculty at all (see Figure 10.6). When broken down by institutional type, it was found that community colleges have a stronger tendency to pay faculty through a load arrangement (see Figure 10.7).

On the very sensitive issue of ownership of intellectual property, two-year institutions also were clearly more likely to claim ownership of distance learning courses (see Figure 10.8). In understanding these data one needs to try to balance the apparently tougher stance of the two-year

Figure 10.6
Faculty Compensation (Question 24) (How are full-time faculty compensated for teaching distance learning format courses?)

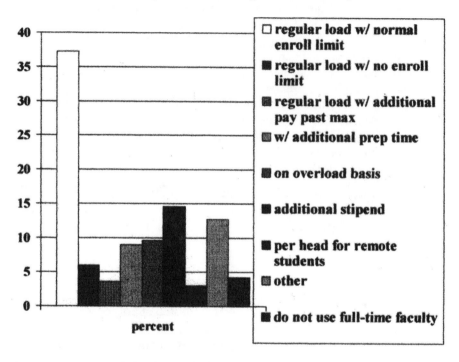

institutions toward faculty with their consistent focus on access, subsidizing of distance learning efforts, and lack of interest in pursuing new forms of revenue. Conversely, one needs to understand how the much higher explicit interest of doctoral degree–granting institutions in increasing revenue through distance learning and in cementing ties to industry matches with their much more lenient policies toward faculty compensation and intellectual property ownership. First, there appears to be much less diversity among community colleges in their policies toward faculty than among doctoral institutions. Second, research institutions are by their nature more likely to have faculty members who are concerned with copyright issues because they are more actively involved in original research than faculty at two-year institutions. Nevertheless, one can't help but wonder if the stricter approach to faculty issues at the community colleges in regard to distance learning isn't part of a larger effort to restructure the teaching workforce and the overall economics of two-year institutions.

One of the most interesting findings in this study is the very complex and diverse approach to distance learning that doctoral degree–granting

Figure 10.7
Faculty Compensation by Institution Type (Questions 2 & 24) (highest degree your institution awards)

Highest degree your institution awards? * How are full-time faculty compensated for teaching distance learning format courses? How are full-time faculty compensated for teaching distance learning format courses? Crosstabulation

		How are full-time faculty compensated for teaching distance learning format courses?									Total
		regular load with normal enrollment limits	regular load with no ceiling on enrollment	regular load with additional pay after seat maximum	with additional preparation time	on overload basis	additional stipend	regular load for in-person class, per head for remote studen	other	do not use full-time faculty	
Highest degree your institution awards? associate	Count	23	3	2	5	5	4		5	1	48
	% within Highest degree your institution awards?	47.9%	6.3%	4.2%	10.4%	10.4%	8.3%		10.4%	2.1%	100.0%
bachelor's	Count	5		2			1	1	2	3	14
	% within Highest degree your institution awards?	35.7%		14.3%			7.1%	7.1%	14.3%	21.4%	100.0%
master's	Count	17	4	1	5	4	8	1	7	2	49
	% within Highest degree your institution awards?	34.7%	8.2%	2.0%	10.2%	8.2%	16.3%	2.0%	14.3%	4.1%	100.0%
doctorate	Count	17	3	1	5	7	10	2	7	1	53
	% within Highest degree your institution awards?	32.1%	5.7%	1.9%	9.4%	13.2%	18.9%	3.8%	13.2%	1.9%	100.0%
Total	Count	62	10	6	15	16	23	4	21	7	164
	% within Highest degree your institution awards?	37.8%	6.1%	3.7%	9.1%	9.8%	14.0%	2.4%	12.8%	4.3%	100.0%

Figure 10.8
Intellectual Property by Institution (Questions 2 & 30) (Highest degree your institution awards?)

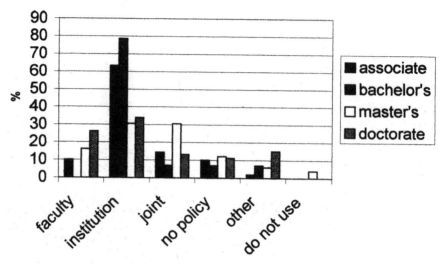

institutions are taking, particularly in relation to faculty issues. One interviewee from a doctoral degree–granting institution talked about extreme changes taking place in the institution in regard to the use of faculty teaching distance learning courses, and its effect on faculty and their control over the university.

> Of course the new school will change everything. Right now we are primarily using our regular faculty. Our first concern will be the quality, and student needs, learner needs, not the institution necessarily, or the faculty necessarily. That's a change. Because the faculty have had a great deal of control of the institution. The students pretty much had to accept everything, but now that has turned, and students have many different options, and we need to follow that turn. . . . In the new school, first offers will go to our regular faculty, but if the faculty member is not available, or not interested in teaching, then we are free to go anywhere else—to other campuses, to outside industry, or anywhere else. (Vice-President, large, independent, urban, eastern U.S. doctoral degree–granting institution)

As a result of corporate administrative approaches, faculty roles in distance learning appear poised to change. Furthermore, the study finds that distance learning is often connected to revenue-seeking activity by who initiated the use and where the activity is administratively housed. Nevertheless, although a revenue-seeking administrative structure was found, evidence of lower academic standards was not apparent in standard course approval and assessment methods. Consequently, the hypothesis that institutions implementing distance learning primarily in order to increase revenue are less likely to have strong academic standards is disproved.

The data in the previous chapter indicated a slightly higher concern for and sophistication in pedagogical approaches for those institutions focusing on access rather than the pursuit of new revenue sources. Figure 10.9 shows that those institutions with an expressed revenue motivation for using distance learning scored slightly lower in every single pedagogical category. Those indicating a revenue motive were slightly less in agreement with the pedagogical focus on interaction and had a slightly lower emphasis on interaction; collaboration as a pedagogical approach was slightly less of interest, and simulations were also less common for them. Those seeking additional revenue also responded less to the question about computer interface navigation issues, and a concentration on a tutorial model with one-on-one interaction.

Figure 10.9
Comparison of Pedagogical Sophistication (Questions 40, 41, 42, 43, 44 & 45)

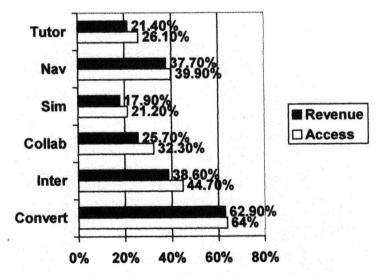

Note: Percentage of responses indicating "strongly agree" in response to questions. Full pedagogical issues labeled as follows: Tutor, Navigation, Simulation, Collaboration, Interaction, Conversion associated with survey questions referenced above.

In turning to the more concrete issues of course development, it is appropriate to ask, How is the course development process affected by a pursuit of revenue? Those institutions motivated by revenue compared with those motivated by access responded more often that they take less than six months to develop a course (70.6% versus 61.8%) and regarded distance learning courses more often as simply automating regular courses (15.9% versus 15.3%). An intriguing statistic is that those concerned with access responded more often that they develop all new course material for a distance learning course than those institutions pursuing additional revenue by a margin of 27.4% to 18.8%. Assessment for those revenue-motivated institutions tended very slightly more to be the same as for traditional courses (87.1% to 86.2%) (see Figure 10.10).

Because these differences are not statistically significant, the hypothesis that there is a connection between institutional motives to increase revenue and a lack of pedagogical sophistication in distance learning format courses is disproved. Nevertheless, while the statistical differences between those institutions pursuing additional revenue and those concerned with access as motivations for distance learning are not significant in relationship to pedagogical concerns, they are broad and consistent. In response to virtually every question aimed at evaluating pedagogical sophistication, revenue-seeking institutions scored slightly lower. Taking such responses individually, one would hesitate to draw conclusions. However, based on the responses as a whole a troubling pattern emerges, in that those institutions involved in distance learning for monetary reasons have less sophisticated and rigorous pedagogical approaches.

In considering why the last two hypotheses connecting the pursuit of revenue with lower academic standards and less pedagogical sophistication

Figure 10.10
Course Development (Questions 6, 47, 48, 49)

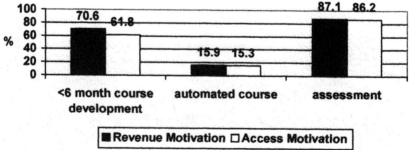
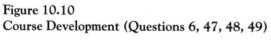

were disproved, one should turn to the surprisingly high use of regular faculty. As indicated in Table 8.1, 76.6% of the respondents reported using only 0–25% adjunct faculty. It is reasonable to conclude that the high use of regular faculty has contributed to stronger academic quality and pedagogical practices. Additionally, the pattern of treating distance learning courses in the same way as traditional courses in terms of other academic processes such as course approval and assessment has undoubtedly also led to higher academic quality. One key question to ask in the future is, Will this similarity in level of quality continue if the use of adjunct faculty is increased greatly? Furthermore, it appears that we are confronted with a bit of a paradox in finding that the academic quality is high because of the use of regular faculty and usual academic processes, while this has possibly also led to a lack of innovation. Distance learning will always be a pale and inferior imitation of the face-to-face experience as long as it sticks to traditional administrative and pedagogical methods.

BEST PRACTICES RECOMMENDATIONS

While it is undoubtedly somewhat dangerous given the newness and controversial nature of distance learning, in conclusion I want to sketch out some best practices strategies for institutions venturing into the use of distance learning.

- Understand Why Distance Learning Is Used at Specific Institutions

The first lesson seen in the data from this study is that it is important for institutions to be clear on why they are using distance learning. It was repeatedly seen that institutions developed distance learning in a haphazard fashion without incorporating it into overall institutional planning. While certainly it is important to test whether the aims of distance learning use fit well with the institutional mission, a more specific understanding of how classroom use of technology fits in with strategic planning is crucial.

- Enter into Agreements with For-Profit Entities with Great Caution

We saw in the interviews that some had begun their use of distance learning by forming partnerships with for-profit entities, but eventually grew out of such agreements. While certainly this is characteristic of a type of organizational learning that needed to take place at institutions, it is important that institutions understand the specific competencies acquired through such relationships, and use these outside relationships for very specific and limited uses.

- If New Revenue Generation Is a Clear Institutional Motivation,
  Understand the Economics

While we saw that many of these institutions claim that they have developed revenue-generating programs, it is clear to practitioners that distance learning in American higher education is not the cash cow often advertised. Institutions with clear and explicit institutional motivations to generate revenue need to understand this and appreciate the specific economics that make this so. A key reason many distance learning programs underperform is that they are modeled too closely on traditional classroom courses. Using regular faculty to teach their usual courses in a similar fashion can only lead to a more, not less, expensive program.

- If New Revenue Generation Is a Clear Institutional Motivation,
  Watch the Quality

Although the data from this study show no significant difference between distance learning and traditional education in academic oversight practices, there is reason to suspect that institutional revenue motivations might lead to sacrifices in pedagogical quality in individual cases. While certainly a simple profit motive does not automatically lead to a sacrifice in quality, it seems to me natural that it might. Administrators venturing down that road are advised to put safeguards in place that ensure quality and ethical behavior.

- Try for More than Automation of the Traditional Classroom

The single greatest problem with distance learning in higher education in America today is that it is usually too tied to traditional models of higher education both administratively and pedagogically. On the administrative end, most programs have developed using usual university administrative structures, including formats, academic oversight, faculty agreements, assessment, outcomes, and requirements for students. On the pedagogical level the situation is even worse. I was struck throughout by the lack of inventiveness or desire to explore new ways of learning exhibited by many of the institutions participating in this study. What could be less pedagogically innovative than simply audiotaping or videotaping classroom lectures? Even in the computer environment, simply digitizing lectures and automating passive learning experiences is hardly a pedagogical revolution. Administrators and faculty need to take the opportunity that new technology offers to rethink how they organize higher education administratively, and how best to serve the growing and diverse population of learners.

- Faculty Compensation and Intellectual Property—Short Agreements; Understand the Economics

Faculty compensation issues are probably the most controversial aspect of the whole topic of distance learning, so I venture an opinion with more than a little reluctance. There are two main problems with this discussion. The first problem is the desire to keep compensation in line with current structures, while at the same time taking advantage of the savings that can come from some distance learning models. The second problem is that both administrators and faculty tend to exaggerate the potential value of their distance learning courses and intellectual property, respectively. Consequently, a recommended good practice at this point is to address these clear problems.

Those interviewed in this study had some useful suggestions, including short copyright agreements (three years or less) and long-term contracting for course developers to update materials as a course custodian. Given the exaggerated expectations regarding long-term revenue from faculty intellectual property, short-term agreements make sense. Although in practice, particularly in the early development stages, they are the same, one needs to separate the course developers from the instructor for specific classes. If the goal is to reduce the expense of instruction, then distance learning must be used to reduce faculty expenses through the development of materials that are substituted for variable faculty costs. For this to work economically would require using less faculty time per course, and/or employing lower-paid tutors instead of regular faculty. Administrators need to be clear here on what their motivation is for utilizing distance learning. If they expect to generate more revenue, they need to key in on the economics of how faculty are used. If offering what is likely to be more expensive courses through distance learning methods makes sense for that institution, then using regular faculty is a clear path.

What I have described above regarding the faculty represents the practical administrative aspects, but does not deal with the larger philosophical issues. My own perspective is that one needs to be very conscious of the different types of higher education institutions, missions, and populations served. For a selective traditional undergraduate program, I would be very hesitant to attempt changing the roles of faculty in order to increase revenue through the use of distance learning. However, in continuing education or adult degree programs, I think that it makes sense to consider changes in faculty roles to make education more affordable if quality can be maintained.

FINAL THOUGHTS

Innis (1991) argued provocatively that dominant societies use communication to reproduce their influence, and consequently the use of a new medium can lead to the emergence of a new civilization. This principle was seen in the rise of the Roman Empire involving the devaluing of the oral tradition and the imposition of writing. However, Innis warned, with the evolution of communication systems come losses and changes in power relationships. He thought that freedom of thought itself was in danger of being destroyed by technology and the mechanization of knowledge. Writing about adult education specifically, he argued that to reach a larger audience, education was following popular media forms such as newspapers and radio, and assuming the methods of advertising. Does the use of distance learning in American higher education signal this kind of significant loss? Is distance learning the epitome of the mechanization of knowledge and the commercialization of education to the point that it is now little more than commercial advertising? Or as John Daniel of the British Open University claims, does it amount to the discovery of the Holy Grail of education: increased access with higher quality? To answer this question more research needs to be done centering on three important areas: new administrative structures, the changing role of the faculty, and pedagogical approaches.

According to Bates (2000b), in order to gain cost-effectiveness, university teaching/learning needs to be substantially restructured toward a "post-industrial form of organization." He, as well as many of those who participated in this study, have argued that the present structure of the university is unsuited to the new forms of technological delivery. Bates claims that this new structure requires partnerships based on complementary competencies. We saw in the literature review that these relationships with industry are at the core of the debate over the commercialization of higher education. These partnerships mean both structural and cultural change and, according to Bates, begin with institutions understanding their own organizational competencies. When an institution understands its own competencies and limitations, the question of going outside for resources arises. This book's research literature review and original research reveal many key questions for institutions considering distance learning, including whether the institution should license courses, use course brokers, and form partnerships with for-profit businesses.

Bowie (1994) argues that academic organizations pursue eternal truth, while business organizations seek a perishable product. How relevant is this distinction in relationship to distance learning? Can universities both pursue truth and produce a commercial product? Partnership formation leads to controversy, but at the same time may help higher education institutions focus more on core competencies, reduce expenses, and improve services. Furthermore, Kidwell, Mattie, and Sousa (2000) argue that the use of new technologies can improve customer service, personalization of services, and the establishment of new relationships with both educational suppliers and key constituents. Nevertheless, we have seen from the arguments advanced in Chapter 4 that such partnerships pose dangers that need to be watched closely.

Furthermore, distance learning and university partnerships with corporations may be changing faculty roles. Slaughter and Leslie (1997) argue that during the industrial revolution, faculty members were able to position themselves between capital and labor. The shift occurred when the corporate search for new products converged with faculty and university searches for increased funding. Restructuring often put increased resources into those departments closest to the market. When the financial condition of higher education worsened in the 1980s, the fiscal uncertainty encouraged faculty and institutions to direct their efforts toward research that intersected with the market. Slaughter and Leslie (1997) argue that financial behavior defines organizational behavior, so that changes in expenditures mean changes in the nature of academic labor.

Probably the largest gap in research concerning distance learning has to do with effective pedagogical approaches. Bates (2000b) sees it as increasingly important to define the purpose and unique features of face-to-face teaching and the role of the physical campus. In order to justify the extra cost of using technology, he believes that distance learning needs to be accompanied by a reorganization of the teaching process. The ultimate goal according to Bates is to improve the quality of learning while increasing cost-effectiveness. There are many areas that future researchers might address regarding the pedagogy of distance learning, but a particularly critical topic is the use of images. Although photographic images and documentary films of various sorts have been utilized in education for many years, there remains an inadequate understanding of the theoretical implications of their use. Now with digital images so prominent in computer-enabled learning, understanding still and moving images in education has become even more important. Issues such as point-of-view, implications of editing and image association, passive versus active positioning, and the psychology of viewing images all need to be better understood. Much of the work done in the last few years in narrative and documentary film criticism is very relevant and useful in regard to this discussion and should be incorporated in the research of the educational application of still and moving images. My own contribution to this research is in another book entitled *The Knowledge Medium: Designing Effective Computer-Based Learning Environments* (Berg, 2002). Furthermore, the extraordinary advances of the past decade in the neurosciences need to be examined for relevance to the search for better utilization of technology in teaching/learning. Surely, in the long run this new knowledge about the human brain will be important in improving distance learning pedagogy.

Clearly, distance learning in higher education is on the rise. The sample for this study from the higher education institutions most involved in distance learning shows a 35.4% increase in the number of distance learning courses offered, from 9,826 in 1998–99 to 13,308 in 1999–2000. One can argue about the reasons for the increased popularity, but one community college representative from this study probably put it best when describing the history of use at her institution:

> The growth of our online program was faculty-driven, president-driven, and then student-driven. (Vivian Sinou, Dean, Distance and Mediated Learning, Foothill College)

Distance learning, we see here, was finally a student-driven phenomenon. However, is popularity enough?

One needs to be concerned about the altered faculty role that distance learning brings. Angelo (2000) believes that academic change efforts often fail because they have not addressed faculty's legitimate reasons for resisting change. Too often in discussions about distance learning, faculty concerns are dismissed quickly because they appear self-interested. However, regardless of their motivation, faculty fears that attempts to increase productivity through distance learning will undermine scholarship and academic freedom may be meaningful. A representative from one of the nation's top research institutions in this study characterized faculty feelings toward distance learning.

> I think that there is in general among faculty a certain amount of suspicion about distance learning, not necessarily ours, but where it is going in general. Not even just for [institution], where is university education going? How will that affect them? (Program Manager, independent, western U.S. doctoral degree–granting institution)

In terms of the adoption of distance learning, the theory that individuals need to perceive the relative advantage of the innovation is an important point in relationship to faculty. According to Rogers (1962), the advantage of an idea can be emphasized by a crisis. Do current economic and demographic pressures, such as "Tidal Wave II" in California (the expectation of huge increases in the number of people wanting to attend college), represent this kind of crisis that can accelerate the need for innovation?

However, opinion leaders and change agents are also important in understanding innovation and change in educational environments. This factor was identified repeatedly in the histories offered by interviewees. According to Rogers (1962), opinion leaders are usually internal to an organization, conform more closely to social system norms than the average member, have higher social status, and are more likely to use external sources of information than their followers. In higher education, this is a description of faculty. Conversely, change agents are generally external to an organization and tend to be effective only when client organizations perceive a need for an innovation before it can be successfully introduced. Both the literature reviews on the nature of change in higher education and the interviews in this book show that faculty are keys in the successful adoption of distance learning. Consequently, the faculty's legitimate concerns about the use of distance learning need to be addressed fully, as well as their false assumptions.

Recently, many authorities have argued that the distinction between distance learning and traditional universities using innovative approaches is becoming less meaningful (Tait & Mills, 1999; Herman & Mandell, 1999; Johnson, 1999; Tait, 1999). Herman and Mandell (1999) point out that nontraditional and traditional colleges are converging in their pedagogies, goals, and student bodies. According to Powell, McGuire, and Crawford (1999), the contemporary student represents a merging of characteristics of the conventional and nonconventional. In looking forward, one of those interviewed expressed a vision for the future of higher education in which the best of distance learning methods and models is incorporated into higher education.

> Actually, I think we are going to evolve to the point where we take "distance" out of learning, out of education. What we are going to do is infuse the methods and models we are learning effectively, and it's just going to be about other ways of teaching and learning, and students are going to have options. (Carole Hayes, Coordinator, External Relations and Development, Office for Distributed and Distance Learning, Florida State University)

The final question that needs to be asked, particularly by public institutions, is about the quality of the access they are offering. Powell, McGuire, and Crawford (1999) argue that making education accessible to a wide population does not necessarily make the system fair. Is the access given by distance learning meaningful? This is a key question for distance learning because the results of exclusion from higher education are increasingly drastic in terms of long-term economic effect, social station in society, and self-image. According to Herman and Mandell (1999), in a knowledge society learning itself becomes a weapon in the competition for money and power. Furthermore, while distance learning is offered as an opportunity, greater access to higher education can in a sense also legitimate inequality. Herman and Mandell argue that what is needed is a true dialogue between these newly served populations and the higher education institutions. Is distance learning the best way for the underserved to gain access? Is it providing access to higher education in an equal manner, or is it only offering a second-rate education in an environment in which it is harder to learn? Furthermore, is the development of distance learning with large promises of access curtailing investment in other, perhaps more effective, ways for underserved populations to gain access? Tait (1999) claims that decision makers need to ask, at the policy level, how is access being supported in distance learning? How is exclusion reasserting itself?

A community college respondent sees distance learning evolving with more generic approaches developing side by side with more ambitious ones.

> The problem is that I don't think very many of them are doing it well. So, I see things shaking out in the next five to ten years. We are going to have people who are going to want to go get a Big Mac, kind of the University of Phoenix approach, and some people will want that. But I also think that there will be a shakeout and some really strong online programs identified, and that's where people will go. (Greg Chamberlain, Dean of Learning Resources, Bakersfield College)

Clearly those involved in distance learning feel that the access they are giving is meaningful and that they represent the strong programs mentioned above. One of the most encouraging findings of this study is the clear pedagogical focus and optimism of institutions regarding distance learning. Institutional representatives (including doctoral degree–granting institutions) widely believe in the pedagogical advantages of distance educational technology (see Figure 10.11). In the next few years we will see if this optimism is justified. This book suggests that while distance learning spreads swiftly in America, educators must be watchful to prevent the motivation to generate much-needed new revenue from interfering with the realization of the pedagogical advantages that new technology offers.

Figure 10.11
Learning Advantages (Question 11)

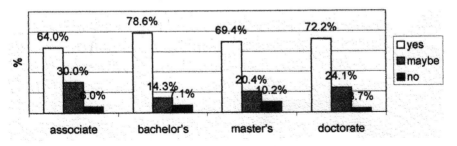

APPENDIX A

Distance Learning Survey

Please fill out the form below and **click the submit button at the end to complete**. Please note: for the purposes of this study, I define distance learning as at least 1/2 reduction in traditional face-to-face teacher-student contact using any delivery method (from mail to email, from videotape to videoconferencing). This survey is designed to be completed by the person most knowledgeable about your institution's distance education course offerings.

Your email address:

Do you speak for the university as a whole in relationship to distance learning?
- ○ Yes
- ○ Maybe
- ○ No

1. Are you (check all that apply):
   - ○ full-time administrator
   - ○ part-time administrator
   - ○ tenured faculty
   - ○ part-time faculty

2. Highest degree your institution awards:
   - ○ Associate
   - ○ Bachelor's

○ Master's

○ Ph.D./Professional degree

3. Your institution is:

○ public

○ independent

4. Number of distance learning format (at least 1/2 reduction in face-to-face student-teacher contact) courses Summer 1999–Spring 2000?:

5. Number of distance learning format courses Summer 1998–Spring 1999?:

Implementation Motive

6. What do you see as the main reason(s) for your institution being involved in offering distance learning format programs? (mark all that apply)

○ provide access to wider student population

○ provide IT skills for students

○ new source of revenue

○ reduce expenses

○ belief in teaching/learning advantages of DL

○ desire to keep up with competition

○ other, please specify:

7. Is providing greater access to student populations part of your institutional mission?

○ Yes

○ Maybe

○ No

8. Do you see providing information technology skills for students as a primary role for your institution?

○ Yes

○ Maybe

○ No

9. Is the pursuit of new sources of revenue for the institution through new program development a primary concern?

○ Yes

○ Maybe

○ No

10. Is the reduction of labor and facility costs a primary force in institutional planning?

○ Yes

○ Maybe

○ No

11. Do you believe that technology offers specific teaching/learning advantages?

○ Yes

○ Maybe

○ No

12. Is it necessary to offer distance learning format courses in order to keep up with competing institutions?

○ Yes

○ Maybe

○ No

13. Who initiated the use of distance learning courses at your institution?

○ top university administrator(s)

○ extended/continuing education dept.

○ individual faculty

○ task force/committee

○ external agency

○ other, please specify:

14. Have the availability of funding sources and/or new state or federal government agencies encouraged the development of your distance learning programs?

○ Yes

○ Maybe

○ No

Administration/Management

15. In what administrative unit is the distance learning program now housed?:

16. Is this administrative unit budgetarily described as:

○ subsidized

○ partial subsidized

○ self-supporting

17. Is there an institutional distance learning plan?

○ Yes

○ No

○ Don't know

If so, who wrote it (position)? If a committee created it, what departments were represented?:

18. Which of the following best describes the current economic status of your distance learning program:
    ○ large deficit
    ○ deficit
    ○ break even
    ○ profit
    ○ large profit

19. Does your institution have a different procedure for the academic approval of distance learning format courses?
    ○ Yes
    ○ No
    If so, how is it different?:

20. Does your institution use whole courses licensed from other educational institutions?
    ○ Yes
    ○ No

21. Are you using any kind of course brokering service to market distance learning courses to non-matriculated students?
    ○ Yes
    ○ No

22. Do you feel that the distance learning program is consistent with your institutional mission?
    ○ Yes
    ○ Maybe
    ○ No

23. Do you view distance learning in higher education as an administrative innovation?
    ○ Yes
    ○ Maybe
    ○ No

24. How are full-time faculty compensated for teaching distance learning format courses:
    ○ As regular load with normal enrollment limits
    ○ As regular load with no ceiling on enrollment
    ○ As regular load with additional pay after seat maximum
    If so, what amount?:
    ○ With additional preparation time

If so how much?:

○   On an overload basis

If so, how calculated?:

○   With additional stipend

If so, what amount?:

○   As regular load for in-person class, per head for remote students

○   Other, please specify:

○   Do not use full-time faculty

25. Are faculty compensated differently for different types of technologies utilized (i.e. videotape versus Internet based)?

○   Yes (please specify difference):

○   No

26. Who determines which faculty/instructor will teach a distance learning course? (check all that apply)

○   The academic department administration

○   The distance education director

○   The faculty/instructor

○   Joint decision between faculty and administration

○   Other, please specify:

27. What form of recognition is there for faculty/instructors teaching distance learning format courses? (check all that apply)

○   Merit reimbursement

○   Promotion

○   Tenure

○   None

○   Other, please specify:

28. Please indicate the level of faculty/instructor training/professional development in relationship to distance learning courses.

○   Available

○   Recommended

○   Required

29. How is training provided? (check all that apply)

○   in person at beginning

○   in person on-going

○   online

○   print

30. When a full-time faculty member develops a distance learning course as part of either regular load, overload, or for a stipend, who owns the intellectual property rights?
    - ○ faculty
    - ○ institution
    - ○ joint ownership
    - ○ no policy on this issue at this time
    - ○ other, please specify:
    - ○ do not use full-time faculty

31. What is the percentage of faculty teaching distance learning courses that are classified as adjunct faculty?
    - ○ 0–25%
    - ○ 26–50%
    - ○ 51–75%
    - ○ 76%+

32. Approximately how many technical support staff per faculty/instructor?:

33. How many instruction design experts available per faculty/instructor?:

34. Are courses typically developed by faculty/instructors through:
    - ○ teams
    - ○ individuals
    - ○ both

35. Do you generally require a proctored test for course completion?
    - ○ always
    - ○ sometimes
    - ○ never

36. Have you done a cost/benefit analysis of distance learning?
    - ○ yes
    - ○ no
    - ○ If so, what does it show?:

Pedagogy

37. Which of the following technologies is used as the primary form of delivery for your distance learning courses?
    - ○ Internet
    - ○ CD-ROM
    - ○ pre-packaged videotape (not live)
    - ○ live video (one-way or two-way)
    - ○ telephone (audio only)

○   print-based

○   other, please speficy:

38. Do you view distance learning in higher education as a teaching/learning innovation?

○   yes

○   maybe

○   no

39. What evidence do you have that students learn effectively in distance learning courses? What does it show?:

Please rate your degree of agreement with the following statements in regard to your general institutional approach to distance learning courses.

40. Questions about how best to convert course material to distance learning format are of great importance.

○   strongly agree

○   agree

○   disagree

○   strongly disagree

41. Courses include significant interaction with other students.

○   strongly agree

○   agree

○   disagree

○   strongly disagree

42. Courses offer opportunity to collaborate with other students on projects.

○   strongly agree

○   agree

○   disagree

○   strongly disagree

43. Courses include simulations and/or case studies.

○   strongly agree

○   agree

○   disagree

○   strongly disagree

44. Great care is taken in understanding how students navigate through the course software.

○   strongly agree

○   agree

○   disagree

○   strongly disagree

45. Courses are like one-on-one tutoring with the faculty member, providing rich and prompt feedback to the students.

○   strongly agree

○   agree

○   disagree

○   strongly disagree

46. Taking a distance learning course at your institution is most like (choose one or more):

○   reading a book

○   watching TV

○   watching a movie

○   listening to the radio

○   talking on the telephone

○   writing letters

47. How long does it generally take to develop a new distance learning format course?

○   less than six months

○   1 year

○   2 years

○   More than 2 years

48. Which of the following most closely reflects the course development process?

○   existing course material automated by technology

○   existing course material automated, with some new material

○   all course material developed specifically for distance learning course

49. Is assessment of student learning similar or the same as in traditional courses?

○   Yes

○   no

50. Additional comments?:

○   I would be available for a follow-up short interview over the phone.

○   Yes

○   no

Thank you for taking the time to complete this survey. Please complete the following form if you would like to receive the results from this project.

>   Name:
>   Address1:
>   Address2:
>   City/State/ZIP:

○   Submit Survey

APPENDIX B

Interview Questions

Qualitative Survey
General Demographic Information

1. Institution Name:
2. Interviewee:
3. Title:

Implementation Motive

4. What do you see as the main reasons for your institution being involved in offering distance learning format programs?
5. Describe the process of implementing the use of distance learning courses at your institution.

Administration/Management

6. Describe the administration and management of distance learning here.
7. What are the key aspects of the formal or informal university distance learning plan?
8. Describe how the academic oversight for distance learning courses is the same or different from traditional courses.
9. What has been your approach to collaborations with for-profit company services?
10. In what ways does distance learning fit the overall mission of your institution?
11. How is the use of faculty for distance learning courses the same or different from in traditional courses?

Pedagogy

12. Describe the technologies you use in your distance learning courses and why you use them.

13. How do you address the issue of student interaction in your distance learning courses?

14. What approaches do you use to develop a sense of community in your distance learning courses?

15. How are case studies and simulations used in your distance learning courses?

16. What is your approach to designing computer user navigation schemes in your courses?

17. What is the development process for new distance learning format courses?

18. How is assessment of student learning different from traditional courses?

APPENDIX C

Cover Email

11/2/2000

Attn: Educators Involved in Distance Learning (please forward within your institution if necessary)

The increased use of distance learning is one of the most controversial subjects in American higher education today. Yet clear and comprehensive information on why and how distance learning is being implemented in higher education is hard to find. By completing the linked survey you can contribute to a better understanding of distance learning in higher education, and receive the results of the study as well.

As part of a dissertation project at Claremont Graduate University, I am conducting research on the implementation and practice of distance learning in higher education. This research focuses on patterns of distance learning administration in higher education, including reasons for adoption and administrative practices.

If you do not feel qualified to complete this survey, please forward it to the person at your institution most knowledgeable about distance learning. If you do not believe that your institution is involved in distance learning of any kind, please reply to this email with that statement.

The survey is completed through a convenient computer form. Simply go to the following url: http://www.webcom.com/exed

Thank you.

Gary A. Berg

APPENDIX D

Email to Interview Subjects

Dear XXXX,

The increased use of distance learning is one of the most controversial subjects in American higher education today. Yet clear and comprehensive information on why and how distance learning is being implemented in higher education is hard to find.

As part of a dissertation project at Claremont Graduate University, I am conducting research on the implementation and practice of distance learning in higher education. This research focuses on patterns of distance learning administration in higher education, including reasons for adoption and administrative practices. I ask that you take the time for a short interview either in person or over the phone.

The interview should take approximately 60 minutes to complete. If you need additional information or would like to discuss the project, please call or email.

I thank you.

Sincerely,

Gary A. Berg

APPENDIX E

Statement of Informed Consent Online

Distance Learning Survey

ONLINE STATEMENT OF INFORMED CONSENT FOR RESEARCH PARTICIPATION

By clicking on "I AGREE" below, I hereby give my consent to participate as a subject in an investigation conducted by Gary A. Berg into distance learning practices in higher education as part of his dissertation research at Claremont Graduate University. I understand that: responses will be kept in strictest confidence, and the results of this project will be coded in such a way that my identity will not be attached in any way to the final data that is produced. In the event that I have any questions, I can contact the researcher, Gary A. Berg. If you agree to participate, please double click here:

I agree

APPENDIX F

Statement of Informed Consent (Interview)

I agree to participate voluntarily in a research study on distance learning in higher education conducted by Gary A. Berg as part of his dissertation project at Claremont Graduate University. The information that I provide will be used to conduct research, the purpose of which is to examine distance learning practices in higher education through the experiences and perspectives of the individuals participating in the study.

I understand that the interview includes questions concerning my beliefs, choices, and life events. The interview should take approximately 30–45 minutes. I may decline to answer any question and/or terminate the interview at any time without any reservation whatsoever. Should I have any questions or concerns about the research or about my participation, the interviewer will address them.

I understand that the interview will be tape recorded. If I myself choose to disclose my participation in this study or any part of the interview or if I authorize the investigators to do so, I will take responsibility for any risk associated with such disclosure. My name will used in publications resulting from this study only if I give my written permission. I will be given the option to disclose my participation in the study and have quotes attributed to me after I have completed the interview. I can also choose to read the transcript of my interview, and then express my wishes on a response form.

I understand that I will receive no payment for my participation in this study.

I have read the consent form and fully understand it. All my questions have been answered. I agree to take part in the study.

_____   Gary Berg_____

Printed name of Participant   Name of interviewer

_____   _____

Signature of Participant   Signature of interviewer

_____

Date

Please mail to:

Gary A. Berg

APPENDIX G

Post-Interview Form

Response Form

Post Interview

1. I give permission to be identified by name when quotes from my interview are used:

   ( ) Yes

   ( ) No

2. I give permission to be identified by name in the complete list of interviewees when you publish the results of the study:

   ( ) Yes

   ( ) No

_____

Printed Name

_____   _____

Signature   Date

APPENDIX H

List of Participating Institutions

Institutions Responding to Survey	Carnegie Classification	State
American Military University	Specialized Institutions	VA
Assemblies of God Theological Seminary	Specialized Institutions	MO
Atlantic Cape Community College	Associate's Colleges	NJ
Bakersfield College	Associate's Colleges	CA
Beaufort County Community College	Associate's Colleges	NC
Boston University	Doctoral/Research U-Ext	MA
Bradley University	Master's Colleges & UI	IL
Burlington County College	Associate's Colleges	NJ
Butte College	Associate's Colleges	CA
California State University, Chico	Master's Colleges & UI	CA
California State University, San Diego	Master's Colleges & UI	CA
California State University, San Marcos	Master's Colleges & UI	CA
California State University, Sonoma	Master's Colleges & UI	CA
Central Piedmont Community College	Associate's Colleges	NE
Central Virginia Community College	Associate's Colleges	VA
Central Wyoming College	Associate's Colleges	WY
Chadron State College	Master's Colleges & UI	NE
Chicago State University	Master's Colleges & UI	IL
City Colleges of Chicago, Washington	Associate's Colleges	IL
Clackmas Community College	Associate's Colleges	OR
Community Hospital of Roanoke Valley	Specialized Institutions	VA
Connecticut College	Baccalaureate Colleges-Lib	CT

Cossatot Technical College	Associate's Colleges	AR
Dallas Baptist University	Master's Colleges & UI	TX
Dallas Theological Seminary	Specialized Institutions	TX
Des Moines Area Community College	Associate's Colleges	IA
Dodge City Community College	Associate's Colleges	KS
Edison State Community College	Master's Colleges & UII	NJ
EDUKAN (consortium)	Associate's Colleges	KS
Emporia State University	Master's Colleges & UI	KS
Florida Agricultural & Mechanical U	Master's Colleges & UI	FL
Florida State University	Doctoral/Research U-Ext	FL
Friends University	Master's Colleges & UI	KS
Genesee Community College	Associate's Colleges	NY
Georgia State University	Doctoral/Research U-Ext	GA
Greenville Technical College	Associate's Colleges	SC
Horry-Georgetown Technical College	Associate's Colleges	SC
Hudson Valley Community College	Associate's Colleges	NY
Iowa Western Community College	Associate's Colleges	IA
Jacksonville State University	Master's Colleges & UI	AL
James Madison University	Master's Colleges & UI	VA
Johnson Bible College	Specialized Institutions	TN
Keiser College	Associate's Colleges	FL
Kellogg Community College	Associate's Colleges	MI
Kennesaw State University	Master's Colleges & UI	GA
Kirksville College of Osteopathic Medicine	Specialized Institutions	MO
Labette Community College	Associate's Colleges	KS
Lackawanna Junior College	Associate's Colleges	PA
Lake Sumter Community College	Associate's Colleges	FL
Lakeland Community College	Associate's Colleges	OH
Lansing Community College	Associate's Colleges	MI
Lehigh University	Doctoral/Research-Ext	PA
Louisiana State University & Agriculture	Doctoral/Research-Ext	LA
Mansfield University of Pennsylvania	Master's Colleges & UI	PA
Marian College	Baccalaureate Colleges-G	IN
Michigan State University	Doctoral/Research-Ext	MI
Midland College	Associate's Colleges	TX
Mid-State Technical College	Associate's Colleges	WI
Minnesota West Community & Technical	Associate's Colleges	MN
Mira Costa College	Associate's Colleges	CA
Mississippi County Community College	Associate's Colleges	AR
Missouri Western State College	Baccalaureate Colleges-G	MO
Mount San Antonio College	Associate's Colleges	CA
Naropa University	Specialized Institutions	CO
Newman University	Master's Colleges & UI	KS
North Arkansas College	Associate's Colleges	AR

North Central University	Specialized Institutions	MN
North Dakota State College of Science	Associate's Colleges	ND
North Iowa Area Community College	Associate's Colleges	IA
Northcentral Technical College	Associate's Colleges	WI
Northeastern University	Doctoral/Research-Ext	MA
Northern Michigan University	Master's Colleges & UI	MI
Nyack College	Master's Colleges & UI	NY
Oklahoma State University	Doctoral/Research-Ext	OK
Open Learning Fire Service Program	Baccalaureate Colleges-G	MD
Palo Alto College	Associate's Colleges	TX
Palomar College	Associate's Colleges	CA
Pellissippi State Technical Comm College	Associate's Colleges	TN
Piedmont College	Master's Colleges & UI	GA
Plattsburgh State University of New York	Master's Colleges & UI	NY
Pratt Community College	Associate's Colleges	KS
Prescott College	Master's Colleges & UII	AZ
Red Rocks Community College	Associate's Colleges	CO
Robert Morris College	Specialized Institutions	IL
Saddleback College	Associate's Colleges	CA
Salt Lake Community College	Associate's Colleges	UT
San Diego City College	Associate's Colleges	CA
Sandhills Community College	Associate's Colleges	NC
Santa Fe Community College	Associate's Colleges	FL
Saybrook Institute	Specialized Institutions	CA
Siena Heights University	Master's Colleges & UI	MI
Southeast Community College—Beatrice	Associate's Colleges	NE
Southern Oregon University	Master's Colleges & UI	OR
Southern Utah University	Master's Colleges & UII	UT
Southwest State University	Baccalaureate Colleges-G	MN
Southwestern Community College	Associate's Colleges	SC
St. Cloud State University	Master's Colleges & UI	MN
St. Petersburg Junior College	Associate's Colleges	FL
State University of NJ, New Brunswick	Doctoral/Research-Ext	NJ
State University of NY—Binghamton	Doctoral/Research-Ext	NY
Stevens Institute of Technology	Doctoral/Research-Int	NJ
Suffolk County Community College	Associate's Colleges	NY
Sussex County Community College	Associate's Colleges	NJ
Taylor University	Baccalaureate Colleges-G	IN
Texas A&M University—Commerce	Doctoral/Research-Ext	TX
Texas Wesleyan University	Master's Colleges & UII	TX
Thomas Edison State College	Master's Colleges & UII	NJ
Tidewater Community College	Associate's Colleges	VA
Tiffin University	Specialized Institutions	OH
Treasure Valley Community College	Associate's Colleges	OR

Troy State University—Dothan	Master's Colleges & UI	AL
University of Alabama	Doctoral/Research-Ext	AL
University of Alaska, Southeast	Master's Colleges & UI	AK
University of Arkansas	Doctoral/Research-Ext	AR
University of Central Florida	Doctoral/Research-Int	FL
University of Charleston	Baccalaureate Colleges-G	WV
University of Colorado—Boulder	Doctoral/Research-Ext	CO
University of Illinois at Urbana–Champaign	Doctoral/Research-Ext	IL
University of Iowa	Doctoral/Research-Ext	IA
University of Louisville	Doctoral/Research-Ext	KY
University of Maine—Fort Kent	Baccalaureate Colleges-G	ME
University of Maine—Machias	Baccalaureate Colleges-G	ME
University of Nebraska—Lincoln	Doctoral/Research-Ext	NE
University of Nevada, Reno	Doctoral/Research-Ext	NV
University of North Dakota	Doctoral/Research-Int	ND
University of Oregon	Doctoral/Research-Ext	OR
University of Pittsburgh	Doctoral/Research-Ext	PA
University of Saint Francis	Master's Colleges & UI	IL
University of Sioux Falls	Master's Colleges & UII	SD
University of South Dakota	Doctoral/Research-Int	SD
University of Southern Mississippi	Doctoral/Research-Ext	MS
University of Tennessee, Knoxville	Doctoral/Research-Ext	TN
University of Vermont	Doctoral/Research-Ext	VT
University of Virginia	Doctoral/Research-Ext	VA
University of Wisconsin—Madison	Doctoral/Research-Ext	WI
Utah Valley State College	Associate's Colleges	UT
Virginia Commonwealth University	Doctoral/Research-Ext	VA
West Texas A & M University	Master's Colleges & UI	TX
West Virginia Northern Community College	Associate's Colleges	WV
West Virginia University	Doctoral/Research-Ext	WV
Western Seminary	Specialized Institutions	OR
Wytheville Community College	Associate's Colleges	VA
York College of Pennsylvania	Master's Colleges & UII	PA
York Technical College	Associate's Colleges	SC

32 anonymous institutions (decided to not use survey coding and remain anonymous)

The 2000 Carnegie Classification includes all colleges and universities in the United States that are degree-granting and accredited by an agency recognized by the U.S. Secretary of Education. The 2000 edition classifies institutions based on their degree-granting activities from 1995–96 through 1997–98.

Doctorate-Granting Institutions

Doctoral/Research Universities—Extensive: These institutions typically offer a wide range of baccalaureate programs, and they are committed to graduate education through the doctorate. During the period studied, they awarded 50 or more doctoral degrees per year across at least 15 disciplines.

Doctoral/Research Universities—Intensive: These institutions typically offer a wide range of baccalaureate programs, and they are committed to graduate education through the doctorate. During the period studied, they awarded at least ten doctoral degrees per year across three or more disciplines, or at least 20 doctoral degrees per year overall.

Master's Colleges and Universities

Master's Colleges and Universities I: These institutions typically offer a wide range of baccalaureate programs, and they are committed to graduate education through the master's degree. During the period studied, they awarded 40 or more master's degrees per year across three or more disciplines.

Master's Colleges and Universities II: These institutions typically offer a wide range of baccalaureate programs, and they are committed to graduate education through the master's degree. During the period studied, they awarded 20 or more master's degrees per year.

Baccalaureate Colleges

Baccalaureate Colleges—Liberal Arts: These institutions are primarily undergraduate colleges with major emphasis on baccalaureate programs. During the period studied, they awarded at least half of their baccalaureate degrees in liberal arts fields.

Baccalaureate Colleges—General: These institutions are primarily undergraduate colleges with major emphasis on baccalaureate programs. During the period studied, they awarded less than half of their baccalaureate degrees in liberal arts fields.

Baccalaureate/Associate's Colleges: These institutions are undergraduate colleges where the majority of conferrals are at the subbaccalaureate level (associate's degrees and certificates). During the period studied, bachelor's degrees accounted for at least ten percent but less than half of all undergraduate awards.

Associate's Colleges

These institutions offer associate's degree and certificate programs but, with few exceptions, award no baccalaureate degrees. This group includes institutions where, during the period studied, bachelor's degrees represented less than 10 percent of all undergraduate awards.

Specialized Institutions

These institutions offer degrees ranging from the bachelor's to the doctorate, and typically award a majority of degrees in a single field. The list includes only institutions that are listed as separate campuses in the *Higher Education Directory*. Specialized institutions include:

Theological seminaries and other specialized faith-related institutions: These institutions primarily offer religious instruction or train members of the clergy.

Medical schools and medical centers: These institutions award most of their professional degrees in medicine. In some instances, they include other health professions programs, such as dentistry, pharmacy, or nursing.

Other separate health profession schools: These institutions award most of their degrees in such fields as chiropractic, nursing, pharmacy, or podiatry.

Schools of engineering and technology: These institutions award most of their bachelor's or graduate degrees in technical fields of study.

Schools of business and management: These institutions award most of their bachelor's or graduate degrees in business or business-related programs.

Schools of art, music, and design: These institutions award most of their bachelor's or graduate degrees in art, music, design, architecture, or some combination of such fields.

Schools of law: These institutions award most of their degrees in law.

Teachers colleges: These institutions award most of their bachelor's or graduate degrees in education or education-related fields.

Other specialized institutions: Institutions in this category include graduate centers, maritime academies, military institutes, and institutions that do not fit any other classification category.

The above definition of classifications quoted directly from Carnegie Foundation for the Advancement of Teaching. (2000). *The Carnegie Classification of Institutions of Higher Education, 2000 Edition*. Electronic data file.

Institutions Participating in Interviews

Bakersfield College, Greg Chamberlain, Dean of Learning Resources and Information Technologies

Bellevue Community College, Thornton Perry, Director of Distance Education

Boston University, Elizabeth Spencer-Dawes, Manager, Distance Learning

California State University, Dominguez Hills, Warren Ashley, Director, Mediated Instruction and Distance Learning

Chapman University, Don Cardinal, Faculty

Florida State University, Carole Hayes, Coordinator External Relations

Foothill Community College, Vivian Sinou, Dean of Distance and Mediated Learning

Nassau Community College, Arthur Friedman, Coordinator, College of the Air

St. Cloud State University, John Burgeson, Dean of Continuing Education

Saybrook Institute, Kathy Wiebe, Admissions Coordinator

Texas Wesleyan University, Joy Edwards, Director of Graduate Studies

University of Alabama, Allan Guenther, Marketing Coordinator, Distance Education

Western Seminary, Jon Raibley, Assistant Director of Lifelong Learning Center

Coordinator, large, public, southern U.S. doctoral degree–granting institution

Faculty and Program Director, historically black college and university

Program Manager, independent, western U.S. doctoral degree–granting institution

Vice-President, large, independent, urban, eastern U.S. doctoral degree–granting institution

REFERENCES

Abbott, L. (1999). Innovation.alt—Implications for education of Burke's "web" theory of innovations, compared to Rogers.' *Proceedings of SITE 99.* Charlottesville: Association for the Advancement of Computers in Education.

Accrediting Commission for Community and Junior Colleges, Western Association of Schools and Colleges. (1999). *1999 distance education handbook.* Retrieved February 19, 2001, from the World Wide Web: http://www.accjc.org/dislearn.htm.

Angelo, T. A. (2000). Transforming departments into productive learning communities. In A. F. Lucas & associates (eds.), *Leading academic change: Essential roles for department chairs.* San Francisco: Jossey-Bass.

Anandam, K. (ed.). (1998). *Integrating technology on campus: Human sensibilities and technical possibilities.* San Francisco: Jossey-Bass.

Arvan, L., Ory, J. C., Bullock, C. D., Burncska, K. K., Hanson, M. (1998). The scale efficiency projects. *Journal of Asynchronist Learning Networks.* Vol. 2, Issue 2.

Baker, S. J. (1999). Building the successful virtual university. Proceedings of EDM 99. Charlottesville: Association for the Advancement of Computers in Education.

Bates, A. W. (1995). *Technology, open learning and distance education.* London: Routledge.

Bates, A. W. (2000a). Giving faculty ownership of technological change in the department. In A. F. Lucas & associates (eds.), *Leading academic change: Essential roles for department chairs.* San Francisco: Jossey-Bass.

Bates, A. W. (2000b). *Managing technological change*. San Francisco: Jossey-Bass.

Berg, G. A. (1999). Community in distance learning through virtual teams. *WebNet Journal: Internet Technologies, Applications & Issues*. Vol. 1, no. 2.

Berg, G. A. (2002). *The knowledge medium: Designing effective computer-based educational environments*. Hershey, PA: Idea Publishing Group.

Bernard, H. R. (1988). *Research methods in cultural anthropology*. Newbury Park, CA: Sage Publications.

Blumenstyk, G. (1998a). Utah's governor enjoys role as a leading proponent of distance learning. *Chronicle of Higher Education*. February 6, p. A23.

Blumenstyk, G. (1998b). Western Governors U. takes shape as a new model for higher education. *Chronicle of Higher Education*. February 6, p. A21.

Bok, D. (1991). Universities: Their temptations and tensions. *Journal of College and University Law*. Vol. 18, no. 1.

Bowie, N. E. (1994). *University-business partnerships: An assessment*. Lanham, MD: Rowman & Littlefield.

Boyer, E. (1984). Introduction. In R. M. Jones & B. L. Smith (Eds.), *Against the current: Reform and experimentation in higher education*, Cambridge, MA: Schenkman Publishing.

California Post-Secondary Education Commission. (1996). Moving forward: A preliminary discussion of technology and transformation in California higher education. Sacramento: CPEC.

California Post-Secondary Education Commission. (1997). Coming of information age in California higher education. Sacramento: CPEC.

Campbell, D. T. & Stanley, J. C. (1966). *Experimental and quasi-experimental designs for research*. Chicago: Rand McNally.

Caplan, J. (2000). Assessing educational quality using student satisfaction. In M. J. Finkelstein, C. Frances, F. I. Jewett & B. W. Scholz (eds.), *Dollars, distance, and online education: The new economics of college teaching and learning*. Phoenix, AZ: ACE/Oryx Press.

Center for Research on Information Technology and Organizations. (1999). The teaching, learning and computing survey. Retrieved February 19, 2001, from the World Wide Web: http://www.crito.uci.edu/tlc/html/tlc_home.html.

Chambers, M. (1999). The efficacy and ethics of using digital multimedia for educational purposes. In A. Tait & R. Mills (eds.), *The convergence of distance and conventional education: Patterns of flexibility for the individual learner*. London: Routledge.

Chute, A., Thompson, M. & Hancock, B. (1999). *The McGraw-Hill handbook of distance learning: An implementation guide for trainers and human resources professionals*. New York: McGraw-Hill.

Clark, B. R. (1998). *Creating entrepreneurial universities: Organizational pathways of transformation*. Great Britain: IAU Press.

Coleman, D. E. (1998). Wilson pushes cyber education in budget. *Fresno Bee.* January 9.

Cook, T. D., Appleton, H., Conner, R. F., Shaffer, A., Tamkin, G. & Weber, S. (1975). *"Sesame Street" revisited.* New York: Russell Sage Foundation.

Cooper, D. E. (1995). Technology: Liberation or enslavement? In R. Fellows (ed.), *Philosophy and technology.* Cambridge: Cambridge University Press.

Council of Regional Accrediting Commissions. (2000a). Guidelines for the evaluation of electronically offered degree and certificate programs.

Council of Regional Accrediting Commissions. (2000b). Statement of the regional accrediting commissions on the evaluation of electronically offered degree and certificate programs.

Cuban, L. (1986). *Teachers and machines: The classroom use of technology since 1920.* New York: Teachers College Press.

Daniel, J. S. (1998). *Mega-universities and knowledge media: Technology strategies for higher education.* London: Kogan Page.

Daniel, J. S. (2000). Can you get my hard nose in focus? Universities, mass education, and appropriate technology. In M. Eisenstadt & T. Vincent (eds.), *The knowledge web: Learning and collaborating on the Net.* London: Kogan Page.

David, J. L. (1994). Evaluating the effects of technology in school reform. In B. Means (ed.), *Technology and education reform: The reality behind the promise.* San Francisco: Jossey-Bass.

Davis, S. & Botkin, J. (1995). *The monster under the bed.* New York: Touchstone.

DeCecco, J. P. (1964). *Educational technology: Readings in programmed instruction.* New York: Holt, Rinehart and Winston.

Dillon, C. L. & Cintron, R. (1997). *Building a working policy for distance education.* San Francisco: Jossey-Bass.

Dun & Bradstreet. (2000). College technology review. Shelton, CT: Market Data Retrieval.

Edwards, R. & Minich, E. (1998). Faculty compensation and support issues in distance education. Washington DC: Instructional Telecommunications Council.

Ehrmann, S. (1998). Using technology to transform the college. In K. Anandam (ed.), *Integrating technology on campus: Human sensibilities and technical possibilities.* San Francisco: Jossey-Bass.

Eicholz, G. & Rogers, E. M. (1964). Resistance to the adoption of audio-visual aids by elementary school teachers: Contrasts and similarities to agricultural innovation. In M. B. Miles (ed.), *Innovation in education.* New York: Teachers College Press.

Eisenstadt, M. & Vincent, T. (eds.). (2000). *The knowledge web: Learning and collaborating on the Net.* London: Kogan Page.

Epper, R. M. (1999). State policies for distance education: A survey of the states. Denver, CO: SHEEO.

Feifer, R. G. (1994). Cognitive issues in the development of multimedia learning systems. In S. Reisman (ed.), *Multimedia computing: Preparing for the 21st century*. Harrisburg, PA: Idea Group Publishing.

Finkelstein, M. J., Frances, C., Jewett, F. I. & Scholz, B. W. (eds.) (2000). *Dollars, distance, and online education: The new economics of college teaching and learning*. Phoenix, AZ: ACE/Oryx Press.

Finkelstein, M. J. & Scholz, B. W. (2000). What do we know about information technology and the cost of collegiate teaching and learning? In M. J. Finkelstein, C. Frances, F. I. Jewett, & B. W. Scholz (eds.), *Dollars, distance, and online education: The new economics of college teaching and learning*. Phoenix, AZ: ACE/Oryx Press.

Fleming, A. M. (1964). *A complete guide to accredited correspondence schools*. New York: Doubleday.

Frasson, C. & Gauthier, G. (1990). *Intelligent tutoring systems: At the crossroads of artificial intelligence and education*. Norwood, NJ: Ablex Publishing Corporation.

Froke, M. D. (1995). Antecedents to distance education and continuing education: Time to fix them. In M. H. Rossman & M. E. Rossman (eds.), *Facilitating distance education*. San Francisco: Jossey-Bass.

Fullan, M. (1993). *Change forces: Probing the depths of educational reform*. New York: Falmer Press.

Goldman, F. & Burnett, L. R. (1971). *Need Johnny read? Practical methods to enrich humanities courses using films and film study*. Dayton, OH: Pflaum.

Gorden, R. L. (1975). *Interviewing: Strategy, techniques, and tactics*. Homewood, IL: Dorsey Press.

Gould, J. E. (1961). *The Chautauqua Movement*. Albany: State University of New York Press.

Green, K. C. (2000). Campus computing 1999: The tenth national survey of desktop computing and information technology in higher education. Encino, CA: Campus Computing Project.

Head, A. J. (1999). *Design wise: A guide for evaluating the interface design of information resources*. Medford, NJ: CyberAge Books.

Healey, J. F. (1999). *Statistics: A tool for social research*. Belmont, CA: Wadsworth Publishing Company.

Hefferlin, J.B.L. (1969). *Dynamics of academic reform*. San Francisco: Jossey-Bass.

Heflich, D. A. & Rice, M. L. (1999). Online survey research: A venue for reflective conversation and professional development. Proceedings of SITE 99. Charlottesville: Association for the Advancement of Computers in Education.

Henry, N. B. (ed). (1943). *The forty-second yearbook of the National Society for the Study of Education: Part 1. Vocational education*. Chicago: University of Chicago Press.

Herman, J. L. (1994). Evaluating the effects of technology in school reform. In B. Means (ed.), *Technology and education reform: The reality behind the promise.* San Francisco: Jossey-Bass.

Herman, L. & Mandell, A. (1999). Towards opening the lifeworld with linking adult higher education systems. In A. Tait & R. Mills (eds.), *The convergence of distance and conventional education: Patterns of flexibility for the individual learner.* London: Routledge.

Hoban, C. F. (1942). *Focus on learning: Motion pictures in the school.* Washington, DC: American Council on Education.

Innis, H. A. (1972). *Empire and communications.* Toronto: University of Toronto Press.

Innis, H. A. (1991). *The bias of communication.* Toronto: University of Toronto Press.

Institute for Higher Education Policy. (1999). *What's the difference? A review of contemporary research on the effectiveness of distance learning in higher education.* Washington, DC: National Education Assocation.

Jewett, F. (1999). A framework for the comparative analysis of the costs of classroom instruction vis-à-vis distributed instruction. Paper presented at Executive Forum on Managing the Cost of Information Technology in Higher Education, sponsored by the New Jersey Institute for Collegiate Teaching and Learning (NJICTL), April 16. Princeton, NJ. Retrieved February 19, 2001, from the World Wide Web: http://academic.shu.edu/itcosts/papers.html.

Jewett, F. (2000). A framework for the comparative analysis of the costs of classroom instruction vis-à-vis distributed instruction. In M. J. Finkelstein, C. Frances, F. I. Jewett, & B. W. Scholz (eds.), *Dollars, distance, and online education: The new economics of college teaching and learning.* Phoenix, AZ: ACE/Oryx Press.

Johnson, S. (1999). Introducing and supporting change towards more flexible teaching approaches. In A. Tait & R. Mills (eds.), *The convergence of distance and conventional education: Patterns of flexibility for the individual learner.* London: Routledge.

Katz, R. N. & Rudy, J. A. (eds). (1999). *Information technology in higher education: Assessing its impact and planning for the future.* San Francisco: Jossey-Bass.

Kent, T. W. & McNergney, R. F. (1999). *Will technology really change education?* Thousand Oaks, CA: Corwin Press.

Kidwell, J. J., Mattie, J. & Sousa, M. (2000). Preparing your campus for e-business. In R. N. Katz & D. G. Oblinger (eds.), *The "E" is for everything: E-commerce, e-business, and e-learning in the future of higher education.* San Francisco, CA: Jossey-Bass Publishers.

Kirkpatrick, D. & Jakupec, V. (1999). Becoming flexible: What does it mean? In A. Tait & R. Mills (Eds.), *The convergence of distance and conventional education: Patterns of flexibility for the individual learner.* London: Routledge.

Kitao, K. (1995). The history of language laboratories: Origin and establishment. ERIC ED381020.

Kovalchick, A. (1999). A grounded theory of instructional design. Proceedings of SITE 99. Charlottesville: Association for the Advancement of Computing in Education.

Lape, D. H. & Hart, P. K. (1997). Changing the way we teach by changing the college: Leading the way together. In C. L. Dillon & R. Cintron (eds.), Building a working policy for distance education. San Francisco: Jossey-Bass.

Lee, J. B. & Merisotis, J. P. (1990). Proprietary schools: Programs, policies and prospects. Washington, DC: George Washington University.

Levine, J. S. (1999). Technology and change in education: Culture is the key. Proceedings of SITE 99, pp. 1660–1663. Charlottesville: Association for the Advancement of Computers in Education.

Lewis, L., Alexander, D. & Farris, E. (1997). Distance education in higher education institutions, NCES 98–062. Washington, DC: U.S. Department of Education, National Center for Education Statistics.

Lucas, A. F. & associates (eds). (2000). Leading academic change: Essential roles for department chairs. San Francisco: Jossey-Bass.

MacKenzie, O., Christensen, E. L. & Rigby, P. H. (1968). Correspondence instruction in the United States. New York: McGraw-Hill.

Maitland, C., Hendrickson, R. & Dubeck, L. (2000). Faculty costs and compensation in distance education. In M. J. Finkelstein, C. Frances, F. I. Jewett, & B. W. Scholz (eds.), Dollars, distance, and online education: The new economics of college teaching and learning. Phoenix, AZ: ACE/Oryx Press.

Marshall, C. & Rossman, G. B. (1989). Designing qualitative research. New York: Sage Publications.

Martin, W. B. (1968). Alternative to irrelevance: A strategy for reform in higher education. New York: Abingdon Press.

Massy, W. F. & Zemsky, R. (1995). Using information technology to enhance academic productivity. A report from a June 1995 Educom Roundtable. EDUCAUSE. Retrieved February 19, 2001, from the World Wide Web: http://www.educause.edu/nlii/keydocs/massy.html.

McKnight, C., Dillon, A. & Richardson, J. (1991). Hypertext in context. Cambridge: Cambridge University Press.

Means, B. (ed.). (1994). Technology and education reform: The reality behind the promise. San Francisco: Jossey-Bass.

Metlitzky, L. (1999). Bridging the gap for the mainstream faculty: Understanding the use of technology in instruction. Dissertation, Claremont Graduate University, Claremont, CA.

Miles, M. B. (ed). (1964). Innovation in education. New York: Teachers College Press.

Miller, R. E. (1998). *As if learning mattered: Reforming higher education.* Ithaca, NY: Cornell University Press.

Mills, R. (1999). Diversity, convergence and the evolution of student support in higher education in the U.K. In A. Tait & R. Mills (eds.), *The convergence of distance and conventional education: Patterns of flexibility for the individual learner.* London: Routledge.

Mitcham, C. & Mackey, R. (1972). *Philosophy and technology.* New York: The Free Press.

Morrison, Theodore. (1974). *Chautauqua.* Chicago: University of Chicago Press.

Mort, P. R. (1964). Studies in educational innovation from the Institute of Administrative Research: An overview. In M. B. Miles (ed.), *Innovation in education.* New York: Teachers College Press.

Mumford, L. (1934). *Technics and civilization.* New York: Harcourt, Brace.

Nanson, S. K. (1989). Influences of the Chautauqua Movement on American higher education. ERIC ED312940.

National Center for Education Statistics. (1997). *Distance education at postsecondary institutions: 1997–1998.* NCES 97–062. Washington, DC: National Center for Education Statistics.

National Education Association (NEA). (1999). Bargaining technology issues in higher education: NEA Higher Education Contract Analysis System (HECAS), 1998–99 version. Higher Education Research Center. Washington, DC: NEA.

National Education Association (NEA). (2000). A survey of traditional and distance learning higher education members. Washington, DC: NEA.

National Postsecondary Education Cooperative (NPEC). (1998). *Technology and its ramifications for data systems: Report of the Policy Panel on Technology.* NCES 98–279. Washington, DC: National Postsecondary Education Cooperative.

Newby, T. J., Stepich, D. A., Lehman, J. D. & Russell, J. D. (1996). *Instructional technology for teaching and learning.* Englewood Cliffs, NJ: Merrill.

Nisbet, R. A. (1971). *The degradation of the academic dogma.* New York: Basic Books.

Noble, D. F. (1989). Technology transfer at MIT: A critical view. Testimony before the House Committee on Government Operations, Subcommittee on Human Resources and Intergovernmental Operations, June 13.

Noble, D. F. (1997). *The religion of technology.* New York: Alfred A. Knopf.

Noble, D. F. (1998). Digital diploma mills: The automation of higher education. *First Monday* (e-journal). Retrieved February 19, 2001, from the World Wide Web: http://www.firstmonday.dk/issues/issue3_1/noble/index.html#author

Noffsinger, J. S. (1942). *The manual of standards for private home study schools.* Washington, DC: National Home Study Council.

Oblinger, D. G. & Katz, R. N. (2000). Navigating the sea of "E." In R. N. Katz & D. G. Oblinger (eds.), *The "E" is for everything: E-commerce, e-business, and e-learning in the future of higher education.* San Francisco: Jossey-Bass.

Osgood, R. E. (1994). The conceptual indexing of conversational hypertext. Dissertation, Northwestern University. Retrieved February 19, 2001, from the World Wide Web: http://www.ils.nwu.edu/.

Papert, S. (1993). *The children's machine.* New York: Basic Books.

Parisot, A. H. (1997). Distance education as a catalyst for changing teaching in the community college: Implications for institutions policy. In C. L. Dillon & R. Cintron (eds.), *Building a working policy for distance education.* San Francisco: Jossey-Bass.

Petre, M., Carswell, L., Price, B. & Thomas, P. (2000). Innovations in large-scale supported distance teaching: Transformation for the Internet, not just translation. In M. Eisenstadt & T. Vincent (eds.), *The knowledge web: Learning and collaborating on the Net.* London: Kogan Page.

Pickover, C. A. (1991). *Computers and the imagination.* New York: St. Martin's Press.

Pittman, V. (1986). Pioneering instructional radio in the U.S.: Five years of frustration at the University of Iowa, 1925–1930. Paper presented at the First International Conference on the History of Adult Education, Oxford, UK, July 14–17. ERIC ED297104.

Plowman, L. (1996). Getting side-tracked: Cognitive overload, narrative, and interactive learning environments. London: Meno Publication, British Open University.

Powell, R., McGuire, S. & Crawford, G. (1999). Convergence of student types: Issues for distance education. In A. Tait & R. Mills (eds.), *The convergence of distance and conventional education: Patterns of flexibility for the individual learner.* London: Routledge.

Primary Research Group, Inc. (1999). The survey of distance learning programs in higher education: 1999 edition. New York: Primary Research Group, Inc.

Pumerantz, R. & Frances, C. (2000). Wide-angle view of the costs of introducing new technologies to the instructional program. In M. J. Finkelstein, C. Frances, F. I. Jewett, & B. W. Scholz, (eds.), *Dollars, distance, and online education: The new economics of college teaching and learning.* Phoenix, AZ: ACE/Oryx Press.

Reeves, F. W., Thompson, C. O., Klein, A. J. & Russell, J. D. (1933). *University extension services.* Chicago: University of Chicago Press.

Rogers, E. M. (1962). *Diffusion of innovations.* New York: The Free Press.

Rubin, H. J. & Rubin, I. S. (1995). *Qualitative interviewing: The art of hearing data.* Thousand Oaks, CA: Sage Publications.

Rudolph, F. (1962). *The American college and university: A history.* Athens: University of Georgia Press.

Rumble, G. & Harry, K. (eds). (1982). *The distance teaching universities*. New York: St. Martin's Press.

Russell, T. (1999). *The no significant difference phenomenon*. Chapel Hill: Office of Instructional Communications, North Carolina State University.

Saettler, P. (1990). *The evolution of American educational technology*. Englewood, CO: Libraries Unlimited.

Sarason, B. (1996). *Revisiting "The culture of the school and the problem of change."* New York: Teachers College Press.

Schank, R. C. (1997). *Virtual learning*. New York: McGraw-Hill.

Schillaci, A. & Culkin, J. M. (eds.). (1970). *Films deliver: Teaching creatively with film*. New York: Citation Press.

Schmuck, R. A. & Runkel, P. J. (1994). *The handbook of organization development in schools and colleges*. Prospect Heights, IL: Waveland Press.

Senge, P. M. (2000). The academy as learning community: Contradiction in terms or realizable future? In A. F. Lucas & associates (eds.), *Leading academic change: Essential roles for department chairs*. San Francisco: Jossey-Bass.

Sheingold, K. & Frederiksen, J. (1994). Using technology to support innovative assessment. In B. Means (ed.), *Technology and education reform: The reality behind the promise*. San Francisco: Jossey-Bass.

Shum, S. B. & Sumner, T. (2000). New scenarios in scholarly publishing and debate. In M. Eisenstadt & T. Vincent (eds.), *The knowledge web: Learning and collaborating on the Net*. London: Kogan Page.

Skinner, B. F. (1964). *The technology of teaching*. New York: Appleton-Century-Crofts.

Slaughter, S. (1990). *The higher learning and high technology: Dynamics of higher education policy formation*. New York: State University of New York Press.

Slaughter, S. & Leslie, L. L. (1997). *Academic capitalism: Politics, policies, and the entrepreneurial university*. Baltimore, MD: Johns Hopkins University Press.

Snowden, B. L. & Daniel, J. S. (1980). The economics and management of small post-secondary distance education systems. *Distance Education*. Vol. 1, no. 1, pp. 68–91.

Sperling, J. & Tucker, R. W. (1997). *For-profit higher education: Developing a world-class workforce*. New Brunswick, NJ: Transaction.

Spille, H. A., Stewart, D. W. & Sullivan, E. (1997). *External degrees in the information age*. Phoenix, AZ: American Council on Education and Oryx Press.

Stutt, A. & Motta, E. (2000). Knowledge modelling: An organic technology for the knowledge age. In M. Eisenstadt & T. Vincent (Eds.), *The knowledge web: Learning and collaborating on the Net*. London: Kogan Page.

Sumner, T. & Taylor, J. (2000). Media integration through meta-learning environments. In M. Eisenstadt & T. Vincent (eds.), *The knowledge web: Learning and collaborating on the Net.* London: Kogan Page.

Tait, A. (1999). The convergence of distance and conventional education: Some implications for policy. In A. Tait & R. Mills, R. (eds.), *The convergence of distance and conventional education: Patterns of flexibility for the individual learner.* London: Routledge.

Tait, A. & Mills, R. (eds.). (1999). *The convergence of distance and conventional education: Patterns of flexibility for the individual learner.* London: Routledge.

Taylor, C. D. & Eustis, J. D. (1999). Assessing the changing impact of technology on teaching and learning at Virginia Tech: A case study. In R. N. Katz & J. A. Rudy (eds.), *Information technology in higher education: Assessing its impact and planning for the future.* San Francisco: Jossey-Bass.

Thompson, J. F. (1973). *Foundations of vocational education: Social and philosophical concepts.* Englewood Cliffs, NJ: Prentice-Hall.

Thorson, M. K. (1999). *Campus-free college degrees: Thorson's guide to accredited distance learning degree programs.* Tulsa, OK: Thorson Guides.

Tracy-Mumford, F. (2000). How states are implementing distance education for adult learners. Washington, DC: National Institute for Literacy.

Twigg, C. (1996). Academic productivity: The case for instructional software. A report from the Broadmoor Roundtable. July 24–25. Colorado Springs, CO.

University Continuing Education Association. (1999). *Peterson's independent study catalog.* Washington, DC: University Continuing Education Association.

University Continuing Education Association. (2000). *Peterson's guide to distance learning courses.* Washington D.C.: University Continuing Education Association.

Veblen, T. (1954). *The higher learning in America.* Palo Alto, CA: Academic Reprints.

Wallhaus, R. A. (2000). E-learning: From institutions to providers, from institutions to learners. In R. N. Katz & D. G. Oblinger (eds.), *The "E" is for everything: E-commerce, e-business, and e-learning in the future of higher education.* San Francisco: Jossey-Bass.

Western Interstate Commission on Higher Education. (1997). Good practices in distance education. Boulder, CO.

Wilms, W. W. (1974). *Public and proprietary vocational training.* Berkeley: Center for Research and Development in Higher Education.

Witherspoon, J. P. (1997). Distance education: A planner's casebook. Boulder, CO: Western Interstate Commission on Higher Education.

Witherspoon, J. P. (1998). Distance education profiles: Fifteen examples of distance education practice. Boulder, CO: Western Interstate Commission on Higher Education.

Worth, S. (1981). *Studying visual communication.* Philadelphia: University of Pennsylvania Press.

Yin, R. K. (1984). *Case study research.* Beverly Hills, CA: Sage Publications.

INDEX

About the Author

GARY A. BERG, Ph.D., is Director of Extended Education and Distance Learning at California State University Channel Islands. Dr. Berg has developed many distance learning courses and programs and has consulted for education and government organizations on the use of distance learning. He is the author of *The Knowledge Medium: Designing Effective Computer-based Educational Environments*, as well as numerous articles on various aspects of educational technology.

WITHDRAWN